T0015299

Light within the Shade

Light within the Shade

800 Years of
Hungarian Poetry

Translated by
Zsuzsanna Ozsváth *and* Frederick Turner

Syracuse University Press

Copyright © 2014 by Syracuse University Press
Syracuse, New York 13244-5290

All Rights Reserved

First Paperback Edition 2022
22 23 24 25 26 27   6 5 4 3 2 1

Musical examples created and provided by William Holab Music.

∞ The paper used in this publication meets the minimum requirements of the American
National Standard for Information Sciences—Permanence of Paper for Printed Library
Materials, ANSI Z39.48-1992.

For a listing of books published and distributed by Syracuse University Press,
visit https://press.syr.edu.

ISBN: 978-0-8156-3362-4 (cloth)
      978-0-8156-1146-2 (paperback)
      978-0-8156-5274-8 (e-book)

Library of Congress has cataloged the hardcover edition as follows:

Light within the shade : 800 years of Hungarian poetry / translated by Zsuzsanna
Ozsváth and Frederick Turner. — First edition.

   pages cm

   Includes index.

   ISBN 978-0-8156-3362-4 (cloth : alk. paper) — ISBN 978-0-8156-5274-8 (ebook)
1. Hungarian poetry—Translations into English.   I. Ozsváth, Zsuzsanna, 1934–
II. Turner, Frederick, 1943–
                                                                    2014011852
   PH3441.E3L54 2014

   894'.5111008—dc23

Manufactured in the United States

To the memory of my parents, Margit Nagy and László Abonyi, who taught me these poems; to the memory of my beloved husband, István, who knew and loved these poems; to my children, Kathleen and Peter, who learned from us these poems; and to Shevy and Gary, Elizabeth, Eliana, Tamar, Nina, and Leora, who will now know these poems.

• • •

To my wife, Mei Lin Turner.

ZSUZSANNA OZSVÁTH holds the Leah and Paul Lewis Chair of Holocaust Studies at the University of Texas at Dallas, where she is also director of the Ackerman Center for Holocaust Studies. In addition, Ozsváth is a member of the Texas Holocaust and Genocide Commission. She has written a number of books and articles, among them *In the Footsteps of Orpheus: The Life and Times of Miklós Radnóti* (2000) and *When the Danube Ran Red* (2010). She has translated into English (with Frederick Turner) the works of some of the great Hungarian poets, publishing *Foamy Sky: The Major Poems of Miklós Radnóti* (1992) and *The Iron-Blue Vault: Selected Poems of Attila József* (1999). Ozsváth and Turner have received one of the Hungarian Academy's highest literary prizes, the Milán Füst Prize, for their translations of the poetry of Miklós Radnóti.

FREDERICK TURNER, Founders Professor of Arts and Humanities at the University of Texas at Dallas, was educated at Oxford University. A poet, critic, translator, philosopher, and former editor of the *Kenyon Review*, he has authored over thirty books, including *The Culture of Hope, Genesis, Hadean Eclogues, The New World, Shakespeare's Twenty-First-Century Economics, Paradise, Natural Religion, Two Ghost Poems,* and *Epic: Form, Content, History.* With his colleague Zsuzsanna Ozsváth, he won Hungary's highest literary honor for their translations of Miklós Radnóti's poetry; he has been nominated for the Nobel Prize for Literature.

Contents

Essays

Preface

The poems presented in this anthology of Hungarian poetry range from "Spring Wind Makes the Water Rise," a medieval flower song, to poems composed in the twenty-first century. While every poem in the selection is recognizable to Hungarian readers as important, the collection contains only a fraction of the major poems in the language. Our aim has been the translation and display of a group of poems, composed over the centuries by some of the greatest Hungarian poets, to demonstrate to English-speaking readers their artistic achievement in Hungarian history and culture, their evolutionary development as a tradition, and their significance within the context of world literature.

The book is simply organized: the translations follow forthwith, in chronological order, with sparse notes as needed. An essay by Zsuzsanna Ozsváth is next, providing historical, biographical, and cultural background for the poets and the poetry. The book concludes with an essay by Frederick Turner on the special thematic and literary qualities of Hungarian poetry, together with some notes on our translation practices.

We have been guided in our work by various considerations. One is that the anthology should be representative not only of the poets' work but their literary era, and that each major era should be given its due. The collection should not be too large, so that readers can take it in as they would any fine collection of poetry and easily recognize the nature of the conversation among the poets across the decades and centuries. Another consideration has been that the translations should be faithful in the literal sense to the originals, while departing no more and no less from the English grammatical and idiomatic practice than the originals do from the Hungarian. We have paid special attention to preserving the musicality of the poems by keeping the meter, rhyme scheme, line length, stanza breaks, and capitalization of the originals. Our translations also replicate to some extent the characteristic language of the period and social background in which the poems were composed, using vocabulary from an equivalent time and place in the history of the English language, so as to preserve the cultural integrity of the poems in their historical context. Above all, we have attempted, within the limits of our abilities, to make the translations good English poems in their own right.

Note: The literary executor of Sándor Weöres's estate refused to grant copyright (on any terms) to our translations of his poems. With great regret we have therefore omitted them from this volume.

Acknowledgments

We are indebted to many people and institutions for their help in the preparation of this book.

We would like to thank Dennis Kratz, Dean of the School of Arts and Humanities at the University of Texas at Dallas, for his encouragement and his support of our publication costs. We are grateful to Mimi and Mitch Barnett, who endowed Zsuzsanna Ozsváth's Leah and Paul Lewis Chair of Holocaust Studies at UT Dallas, for their extraordinary help and interest in our work, and for the contribution of the Lewis chair to publication costs. The Founders of the University of Texas at Dallas deserve grateful memory for their ongoing support of the work of Frederick Turner. His Founders Chair also helped support publication costs.

Our thanks are due to Miklós Vajda, who gave us essential advice that helped us bring this work to completion; to Eszter Dallos, who was an invaluable guide in our inquiries; and to Ivan and Mari Abonyi, for their hospitality in Hungary during our research into these poems.

We also wish to express our deepest gratitude to Mei Lin Turner, without whose reading, feedback, care, and advice this manuscript would not have seen the light of day. Her work with the manuscript has been indispensable to the completion of this volume.

Some of the translations in this collection have appeared in the following publications:

Miklós Radnóti, *Foamy Sky: The Major Poems of Miklós Radnóti*, trans. Zsuzsanna Ozsváth and Frederick Turner (Princeton: Princeton University Press, 1992).

The Colonnade of Teeth: Modern Hungarian Poetry, ed. George Gömöri and George Szirtes (Newcastle, UK: Bloodaxe Books, 1996).

The Lost Rider: A Bilingual Anthology. The Corvina Book of Hungarian Verse (Budapest: Corvina Books, 1997).

Attila József, *The Iron-Blue Vault: Selected Poems*, trans. Zsuzsanna Ozsváth and Frederick Turner (Newcastle, UK: Bloodaxe Books, 1999).

Anna T. Szabó and Mónika Masterházi, *Modern Classics from Hungary* (Budapest: Hungarian Book Foundation, 2000).

"End of September." Sheet music lyrics with setting by Denes Agay (New York: Yorktown Music Press, 2003).

Without Knocking. Catalog for an exhibit of paintings by Janet Brooks Gerloff based on the poems of Attila József, Hungarian Embassy, Berlin (February 25–March 18, 2005); Museum of Fine Arts, Budapest (April 12–June 12, 2005); Museum Zinkhütter Hof, Aachen (September 26–November 25, 2005).

The Hungarian Quarterly.

Judaism.

Poetry.

Trinacria.

The translators wish to express their gratitude to these publishers for their service to Hungarian poetry.

Selection of Poems

"Spring Wind Makes the Waters Rise";

medieval Moldavian flower song

Spring wind__ makes the wa - ters rise,__ my flow - er, my__ flow - er.
Who then__ is my choice to__ be?__
Green rib - bons make a light at - tire,
But the__ veil's a heav - ier__ weed,

Ev' - ry__ bird a mate must choose, my flow - er, my flow - er.
I'll choose you and you'll choose me,__
Blown by the winds at its de - sire,__
Weighed it__ is with pain in - deed,__

ANONYMOUS

Spring Wind Makes the Waters Rise
Medieval Moldavian flower song

Spring wind makes the waters rise,
My flower, my flower.

Every bird a mate must choose,
My flower, my flower.

Who then is my choice to be,
My flower, my flower?

I'll choose you and you'll choose me,
My flower, my flower.

Green ribbons make a light attire,
My flower, my flower;

Blown by the wind at its desire,
My flower, my flower;

But the veil's a heavier weed,
My flower, my flower—

Weighted it is with pain indeed,
My flower, my flower.

"Be My Star, Ferryman";

fourteenth–century ballad, eighteenth–century Rákóczy song

Be my star fer - ry - man, bear me o'er the Dan - ube!
Be my star fer - ry - man, bear me o'er the Dan - ube!
Be my star fer - ry - man, bear me o'er the Dan - ube!

This fleece coat I'll give thee, that my Lord has left me!
This fine horse I'll give thee, that my Lord has left me!
This fair self I'll give thee, that my Lord has left me!

No, I will not bear you o'er: Hear the i - cy Dan - ube roar,
No, I will not bear you o'er: Hear the i - cy Dan - ube roar,
Yes, I will then bear you o'er: On a steed with gold - en hair.

Hear the i - cy Dan - ube roar.
Hear the i - cy Dan - ube roar.
And em - brace thee on the shore.

Be My Star, Ferryman . . .

Old Hungarian folk song

Be my star, ferryman, bear me o'er the Danube!
This fleece coat I'll give thee, that my lord has left me!
No, I will not bear you o'er: hear the icy Danube roar,
Hear the icy Danube roar!

Be my star, ferryman, bear me o'er the Danube!
This fine horse I'll give thee, that my lord has left me!
No, I will not bear you o'er: hear the icy Danube roar,
Hear the icy Danube roar!

Be my star, ferryman, bear me o'er the Danube!
This fair self I'll give thee, that my lord has left me!
Yes, I will then bear thee o'er, on a steed with golden hair,
And embrace thee on the shore!

"Getting Down to Living";

old Hungarian charivari song

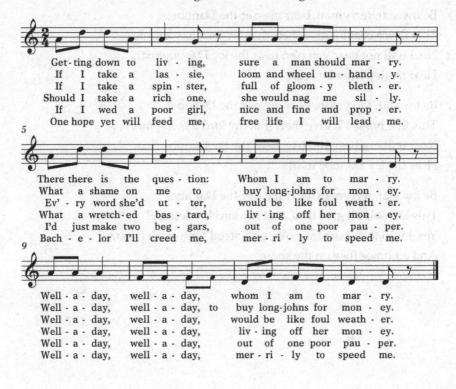

Get-ting down to liv - ing, sure a man should mar - ry.
If I take a las - sie, loom and wheel un - hand - y.
If I take a spin - ster, full of gloom - y bleth - er.
Should I take a rich one, she would nag me sil - ly.
If I wed a poor girl, nice and fine and prop - er.
One hope yet will feed me, free life I will lead me.

There there is the ques - tion: Whom I am to mar - ry.
What a shame on me to buy long-johns for mon - ey.
Ev' - ry word she'd ut - ter, would be like foul weath - er.
What a wretch-ed bas - tard, liv - ing off her mon - ey.
I'd just make two beg - gars, out of one poor pau - per.
Bach - e - lor I'll creed me, mer - ri - ly to speed me.

Well - a - day, well - a - day, whom I am to mar - ry.
Well - a - day, well - a - day, to buy long-johns for mon - ey.
Well - a - day, well - a - day, would be like foul weath - er.
Well - a - day, well - a - day, liv - ing off her mon - ey.
Well - a - day, well - a - day, out of one poor pau - per.
Well - a - day, well - a - day, mer - ri - ly to speed me.

Getting Down to Living

Old Hungarian charivari song

Getting down to living,
Sure a man should marry;
Then there is the question
Whom I am to marry;
Welladay, welladay,
Whom I am to marry.

If I take a lassie,
Loom and wheel unhandy,
What a shame on me
To buy long johns for money,
Welladay, welladay,
To buy long johns for money.

If I take a spinster,
Full of gloomy blether,
Every word she'd utter
Would be like foul weather,
Welladay, welladay,
Would be like foul weather.

Should I take a rich one,
She would nag me silly,
What a wretched bastard,
Living off her money,
Welladay, welladay,
Living off her money.

If I wed a poor girl,
Nice and fine and proper,
I'd just make two beggars
Out of one poor pauper,
Welladay, welladay,
Out of one poor pauper.

God, O God, what shall I
Choose, to not miscarry?
Should I be a bachelor,
Or should I marry?
Welladay, welladay,
Or should I marry?

One hope yet will feed me,
Free life I will lead me,
Bachelor I'll creed me,
Merrily to speed me,
Welladay, welladay,
Merrily to speed me.

Eighteenth- to nineteenth-century

BÁLINT BALASSI (1554–1594)

On Finding Julia, He Greeted Her Thus:
(Sung to the Turkish tune "Gerekmez bu Dünya sensuz")

All the world to me is nothing
If I have thee not, my dearling,
Loveliness with lover meeting;
Health be to thy soul, my sweeting!

Joy thou art to my heart's sadness,
Blessings of a heavenly witness,
Balm of soul's desirous madness,
All God's peace and all its gladness.

Precious fortress, fastness dearest,
Crimson rose of perfume rarest,
Violet daintiest and fairest,
Long be the life thou, Julia, bearest!

As a sunrise thine eyes' dawning
Under coal-black brows a-burning
Fell upon mine own eyes' yearning,
Thine, whose life is my life's morning.

With thy love my heart's afire,
Thou, the princess of my prayer,
Heart and soul and love entire,
Hail, my soul's one last desire!

Finding Julia I, enchanted,
Greeted her as here presented,
Bowed in reverence unwonted,
But a smile was all she granted.

1588–1589

A Soldier's Song

In Laudem Confiniorem

(To the melody of "Only Sorrow")

Knights-at-arms, tell me where there is a place more fair
    than the far fields of the Pale?
When soft is the springtime, sweet the birds' singtime,
    over the hill and the dale;
All in heaven's favor receive the sweet savor,
    dewdrop and meadow and vale.

And the knight's heart is stirred by the fire of the word
    that the haughty foe draws near,
Pricked to more merit by the spur of his spirit,
    goes to his trial with good cheer;
Wounded yet ready, though his brow be all bloody,
    seizes and slays without fear.

Scarlet the guidons, bright heraldry gladdens
    on surcoat and standard below,
In the vanguard he races, the field's vast spaces
    courses, like wild winds that blow;
Gaily caparisoned, bright helms all garrisoned,
    plumed in their beauty they go.

On Saracen stallions they prance in battalions,
    hearing the blast of the horn,
While those who stood guard when the night watch was hard,
    dismounted, rest in the dawn:
In skirmish and night-fray unending well might they
    with watching be wearied and worn.

For the fame, for good name, and for honor's acclaim,
    they leave the world's joys behind,
Flower of humanity, pattern of chivalry,
    to all, the pure form of high mind;

And as falcons they soar over fields of grim war,
    unleashed to strike in the wind.

When they see the bold foe, in joy they Hollo!,
    cracked lances fly end over end,
And if things fall out ill in the field of the kill,
    rally without a command,
And mired in much blood oftentimes they make good,
    drive their pursuit from the land.

The great plains, the forest, the groves at their fairest,
    are their castle, so they deem;
The ambush at woodways, the struggle, the hard days
    are their groves of academe;
Their hunger in battle, the thirst, the hot rattle,
    pleasures to them well beseem.

Their joy in their labor's the blade of their sabers,
    the skull-splitting edge they try;
And bloody and wounded, and many confounded
    in battle, silent they lie;
And the beast's maw full often, and the bird's, is the coffin
    of those who in courage must die.

Young knights of the marches, no shame ever smirches
    the glory that ever is yours,
Whose fame and good name the world will acclaim
    to its farthest and noblest shores;
As the fruit to the tree, may Providence be
    a blessing to you in the wars!

1589

He Supplicates the Lord to Protect Him in His Exile and Extend to Him His Further Blessings

(To the melody of "Ancient Lamentations")

O loving God and kind, in whose mighty hand
    I placed my existence,
Watch over my days, lead me in my ways,
    Thou art all my substance.

Since I was a child, Thou alone I held
    all my hope and staying;
As a son out-clepes in his father's steps,
    I walked ever praying.

Again only in Thou all my trust lies now,
    in my hope and frailty,
And on Thee would lean, and unto Thy reign
    I have pledged my fealty.

What would it Thee boot if in peril's doubt
    I should be corrupted,
Him whom Thou hast won through Thy blessed Son
    as Thine own adopted?

Heed the humble claim on Thine own great name,
    this my supplication,
Show Thy charity, and benignity,
    in my fair good fortune.

Vouchsafe my desire, this my trusting prayer,
    all Thy goodness grant me,
Bless this head of mine, whose whole faith is Thine,
    in my steps prevent me!

As that fairest dew, that Thou sprinklest new
    on the springtime blossom,
Scatter now for me Thy sweet charity
    on Thy servant's bosom.

That, till death destroy, my heart full of joy
    magnify Thy story,
This before all things, this above all things,
    bless Thy name of glory.

This prayer writ by me by the Western Sea,
    Oceanus' shore:
Fifteen hundred years had gathered to their tears
    one and ninety more.

1591

Bitter, As I Know Too Well . . .

Bitter, as I know too well, was my beginning;
Bitter was the orphaned course of my upbringing;
Bitter, sad, would be the time of my wing-taking;
Bitter till I die my heart will go on aching.
Since my heart with sadness as in smoke is smothered,
I, as if a thing, to fate and chance being tethered,
To a cruelty self-renewing and unwithered;
Pain burns on in me, unlucky and unmothered.

1681–1683

VITÉZ MIHÁLY CSOKONAI (1773–1805)

A Restrained Plea

Love's vast passion, all-consuming,
Sears me with its blazing power;
You're the balm to heal my bleeding,
Little *Tulip*, pretty flower:

Eyes, so lovely in their flashing,
Living fire of dawn's first light,
Dewy lips that put a thousand
Griefs and worldly cares to flight.

Grant your lover the angelic
Words that I will hold in awe:
I will pay for them a thousand
Kisses of ambrosia.

1803

The Vow

As your charms have sweetly bound me,
Lovely Lilla! to confound me,
Thus I make my solemn vow:
Since that time no other maiden,
Arrow, flame, so passion-laden,
Shall my faithful heart allow.

This I swear; my adoration
Is the rite of a religion,
Tenets I shall ne'er betray.
That your heart in vows as holy
You might bind to my heart solely,
Angel, sick with hope I pray.

On your snow-white hand I swear it,
By your rose-lips', fire-eyes' merit,
That you'll be my only one.
Whiles I live I swear I'll never
Traffic with another lover:
Lili shall be mine—or none.

1803

To Hope

Heavenly illusion,
Playing with the Earth,
Godlike to the vision,
Hope, blind gift of dearth!
You whom the unhappy,
For an angel guide,
Fashion in a copy,
Pray to unreplied.—
Why does your soft smile so promise
What you cannot give?
Why let drip this joy dishonest
Into where I live?
Stay, O flattering sweetness,
For your own sweet sake;
I believed your witness:
Vows that you would break.

Blooming with narcissus
You my garden set;
Fed with brooks' soft kisses
Lilacs violet;
Thousand-flowered blessings
You beshowered on me,
Heavenly caressings
Spiced their ecstasy.
Every morning my reflections
Like a busy bee
Rode the breezes' indirections
To the fresh rose-tree.
One thing yet was lacked for
In my joys so free;
Lilla's heart I asked for;
Heaven gave it me.

Ah, but my fresh roses
Withered all away;
Springs and greeny closes
Turned to sere and grey;
All my springtime madness
Winter grief now stings;
That old world of gladness
Flew on worthless wings.
If but Lilla you had left me
I should feel no wrong;
No complaint that you bereft me
Should weigh down my song.
In her arms those sorrows
I could all forget,
Pearl wreaths, glad tomorrows,
I should not regret.

Leave, vain hope, O leave me,
Leave me while you may,
Callousness shall sleeve me
In its icy clay.
Doubt, now at its direst
Saps my strength and mirth,
Tired soul seeks its sky-rest,
Body seeks its earth.
Now the scorched vales and the meadows
Lie defaced with blight;
Barren groves now sunk to shadows
With the sun in night.—
Piping philomelas!
Dream-tints in the eye!
Pleasures! Hopes! Sweet Lillas!
Good-bye, good-bye, good-bye!

1803

The Black Wax Seal

Black seal on my truelove's letter,
  Loose at last what you conceal!
Show to my sad head your matter;
  Life, or death, will you reveal?
Make or break—
Lord, I shake!

Shake! Perhaps her rose-stem's smitten
  By a pain that tears her heart,
Or her grief—or death!—are written
  In the dead black of your art.
Does she save
Me a grave?

In a grave? or loves another?—
  Hurls me from her heart's demesne,
A death-sentence to her lover?
  That is what the seal must mean.
It's no lie.
I must die.

I must die but ere I'm buried,
  Open, black and mourning seal!
There might be a word you carried
  That my dying heart might heal,
And your breath
Speak no death.

Speak no death! Ah beg your pardon,
  Letter sweet, with lying seal.
Just "I love you" was your burden,
  Dear redemption, dear repeal:
Sentence, kiss:
Heaven's bliss.

Blissful letter, little treasure!
   Now I kiss you in return;
Lilla's soul was in your measure,
   Lit my day with your new sun,
Healed my heart
With your art.

1803

DÁNIEL BERZSENYI (1776–1836)

Winter Is Coming

Now wilts our verdant park, its sweet adornments fall;
Swept through its naked boughs rustle the yellow leaves,
Roses fled from the maze, and with his balmy scent
Zephyr no longer is blowing.

Mute is the chorus; stilled, in the arbor's green shade,
The wet sally-gardens, the turtledove's cooing.
The dell of the violets does not perfume the air,
Crude sedge clogs the stream's bright mirror.

Silent darkness broods in the mountains' great arches,
The clusters of scarlet berries no longer smile.
Here erstwhile rang out the sweet song of happiness:
All now is sad and desolate.

Oh, how swiftly has winged time suddenly flown away,
All its works afloat round its vanishing feather!
All is appearance, everything under the sky
Fades, as does a forget-me-not.

Slowly the buds of my garland wither and fall,
My beautiful spring has passed me by; just a taste
Touched my lips, I scarcely had time to celebrate
But one or two of its blossoms.

It leaves me and never returns, my golden age;
It cannot be summoned back by any new spring!
Nor can the spell be lifted, my closed eyes opened
By my Lolli's soft brown eyebrow!

Circa 1804

Supplication

God! Whose thought is beyond the wit of the wise,
Glimpsed only by the secretly yearning soul,
    Sunlike your being illuminates, but
        Our eyes cannot stare at its burning.

The Uranean vaults of the high-sphered aether
That revolve about you in their slow order;
    The invisible animalcules:
        Equally miracles of your wise hands.

You brought forth the cosmos' thousand varieties
From nothingness and void; your measureless brow
    Can make and unmake a hundred worlds
        And measure the mighty rivers of time.

Zenith and Nadir praise and glorify you.
The groaning struggle of tempests, the lightning's
    Skyfire, dewdrops, flowers' delicate scapes
        Blazon forth your manifold handiwork.

Ardently I fall before you, Glorious One!
Then when my soul will rise from its shackles and
    Be admitted unto your presence,
        All that it yearns for, it will find at last.

Until that day I shall dry my tears and go
Upon the errands of my calling, seeking
    What paths of the best and noblest souls
        My tendons' strength will suffer me to take.

Secure in my faith I face my grave's deep night!
A stark place, but Oh! it cannot be evil,
    Because it is your work; and my bones
        Though scattered, your loving hands will cover.

1807–1808, 1810

FERENC KÖLCSEY (1790–1838)

Hymn

From the stormy centuries of the Hungarian people

Grant each Magyar soul, O Lord,
Blessings in profusion;
Lend your arm of love and ward
In dark war's confusion.
Bring a year of joy at last
To our wounded nation,
That for future as for past
Has done expiation!

To your cragged Carpathians
You our fathers guided;
And to Bendeguz's sons
Homeland sweet you ceded.
And where Tisza, Duna foam,
Roaring in their gorges,
Arpad's seed bursts into bloom
From heroic forges.

You on the Cumanian plains
Spread our cornfields blowing,
Sprinkled Tokay's purple vines
With your nectar glowing.
O'er the wild Turk's trench you tied
Oft our planted banner;
Under Matthias' grim troops sighed
The proud forts of Vienna.

Ah, but wrath upon our faults
In your bosom blazing,
Lashed the clouds with lightning bolts,
Thunderstrokes amazing;

Now the ravening Mongol's shaft
You let howl upon us,
Now, yoked like a beast of draft,
Turkish masters own us.

Oft indeed upon the tongue
Of the Osman heathens
Clanged their harsh victory-song
O'er our bone-heaped legions!
Worse, O country, 'gainst your breast
Rose your own sons often,
You, by your seed's rebel quest,
Turned your own seed's coffin.

In a cave the fugitive
Fled the sword that sought him;
Nowhere sees he home to live
In the land that wrought him.
Up the cliffs and down the dales
Doubt and sorrow dog him;
At his feet a blood-tide flails,
Fiery seas befog him.

In this fortress, now heaped stones,
Where once joy went winging,
Lamentation, rattled bones
Are the only singing.
Dead men's blood feeds not the free
Flower of our achieving;
Hot tears fall from the yoke-tree
Of our orphans' grieving!

Pity Magyar souls, O Lord,
Racked to dissolution,
Stretch your arm, of love and guard
O'er their pain's dark ocean.

Bring a year of joy at last
To your wounded nation,
That for future, as for past,
Has done expiation!

1823

MIHÁLY VÖRÖSMARTY (1800–1855)

Declaration

To your dear land unswervingly
O Magyar, still be true;
Your cradle once, your grave to come,
That feeds and covers you.

In that great world beyond our pales
You find no place to lie;
Blessed or beaten by fate's hand,
Here you must live and die.

This is the soil on which so oft
Your fathers' blood has flowed,
This, on which every sacred name
A thousand years bestowed.

Here Árpád's hosts fought for our sake,
The bravest of the free;
Here Hunyadi's strong arm broke the yoke
Of bitter slavery.

Freedom! your bloodied flag they bore,
Never to bow or yield;
And here our best ones gladly fell
On the grim battlefield.

And through such great calamity
And after such great strife,
Wounded but yet unbroken held
The nation's home and life.

O greater world of human beings!
To you we bravely cry:
"The suffering of a thousand years
Calls us to live or die!"

It cannot be, so many hearts
Should shed their blood in pain,
So many true and loyal breasts
Break, for their land, in vain.

It cannot be, that so much mind,
Such store of holy will,
In vain should wither, weighted down
Under the curse of ill.

It still must come, it still will come,
A better age, wherefore
Upon a hundred thousand tongues
Their ardent prayers implore.

Or it will come if it must come,
A splendid death and good,
Where round a solemn funeral stands
A nation in its blood.

And people gather by the grave
Where a great nation fell,
And in a million grieving eyes
The tears of mourning swell.

To your dear land unswervingly
O Magyar, still be true;
Your cradle once, your grave to come,
That feeds and covers you.

In that great world beyond our pales
You find no place to lie;
Blessed or beaten by fate's hand,
Here you must live and die.

1836

Night and Star

I am night, you're starlight,
Glittering and chill,
I am dark with anguish,
Desire makes me ill.

Under you my midnight
Quivers painfully,
While your high face hovers
As divinity.

In your beauty's lightrays
Sleep can never flow,
I in waking torment
Dream towards your glow.

Would that I could show you
That which faith keeps hid,
Earthchild's lovely secrets,
To the stars forbid,

What no lips could ever
Breathe out in a vow,
Mystery that only
Night and pain can know.

Would I could uplift this
Mournful face of mine
That my shade might make your
Glory brighter shine.

And the more I blacken
In my throttled pain
So the more you'd kindle
Purer yet again.

Would I might be lost there,
Where I most desire,
Once, but once, to touch it,
Your unquenching fire!

1841

Mankind

1.

Listen. For the singing must be still:
Now the world speaks plain.
Hot wings of the rainstorm turn to chill,
Frozen the wind and rain—
The rain is tears, is sorrow's smart,
The wind sighed by the human heart:
It makes no difference—spirit, virtue, sin:
All hope is vain!

2.

You have heard the story: humankind
Born of their fathers' breath,
Reaped what their fathers sowed and as they sinned,
Inheritance of death:
And the survivors howl for Law,
And law in turn kills many more,
The best have failed, the worst's plots reign:
All hope is vain!

3.

Then the heroes came, and they bestrode
The law with their bright blaze.
Work began: steel cut its bloody road!
Mankind gloried in self-praise.
And when its heroes died, again
It mauled itself in its great pain.
The news? Lightning upon a darkling plain:
All hope is vain!

4.

There is a long peace, and humankind
Teems grossly to beget,
So the plague perhaps may one day find

A grander banquet set.
With greedy eyes it scans the sky:
Earth's not its own, that's why,
The Earth's as hard as grave-ground for this strain:
All hope is vain!

5.

How fertile is the earth, and human hands
Make it more fertile still,
Yet poverty stalks over all the lands
And bondage stamps its will.
Must it be so? Or if not, why
Must ancient times repeat the cry?
What's lacking? Is it virtue? power? Again
All hope is vain!

6.

A godless contract binds you in its bans,
Reason and evil will!
You nourish with the rage of ignorance
Your armies to the kill.
Reason or rage, devil or beast,
Whoever wins, men die at least:
This mud run mad, this god-faced knot of pain!
All hope is vain!

7.

Beneath Mankind the good earth groans, and now
War years and peace years burn.
The curse of brother-hate blooms on its brow:
You'd think that it would learn,
But then it spawns some greater sin.
Humans are dragon-teeth, the strain
Of Man's the dragon-toothed, the race of Cain:
All hope is vain! All hope is vain!

1846

JÁNOS ARANY (1817–1882)

The Mother of Matthias

Elsabeth
Szilágyi
Signs and seals her letter;
Tenderly
Spends on it
Tears both sweet and bitter.

To the high
Town of Prague
She has marked her letter:
Good news sends
To her son
Under lock and fetter:

"Dearest child!
From high Prague
Let them not remove you;
Ransom I
Send for you,
For I dearly love you.

"Silver, gold,
Silver, gold,
I will send to free you;
In my heart
Is your home
Where I long to see you.

"Do not move,
Do not stir,
Orphan, O beware you!
Who shall be

Son to me
If their *plots* ensnare you?

"Let this word
Be conveyed
To Matthias Hunyadi,
To his own
Very hand,
But otherwise, nobody."

She has pressed
In black wax
Seals and appertainers;
Leaning on
Elbow rests
Wait now her retainers.

"Who will bring
With most speed
To high Prague this paper?
A hundred gold,
A good bay horse,
For his body's labor."

"I will go,
I will go,
Seven days shall speed me."
"Seven years
Shorter were
So my soft heart bleed me."

"I will go,
I will go,
Three days brings an answer."
"Three whole months
In my heart
Were a shorter span, sir."

"Lord above,
Lord above,
Give me wings a-burning,
That I might
Swifter fly
Than a mother's yearning."

And behold,
And behold,
Comes a great black raven;
Hunyadi's
Shield and arms
Bear its like engraven.

Down it swooped,
Down it dropped,
From the storm's black turning,
And it plucked
From her hand
Those same words of warning.

"Quick, the bird . . .
Take it back
From the winds of heaven."
See them run,
Bow and gun,
Seek to shoot the raven.

Birds well more
Than five score
Fall now to the catcher;
Not a quill,
Not a trace
Of the letter-snatcher.

Late that night
Through the woods

They pursued the matter:
Midnight came,
And a tap
At the widow's shutter.

"Who knocks there?
What knocks there?
It is the black raven!
Can it bear
The letter there,
Or its like, engraven?

"Red, O red,
Is its seal;
Fine, fine is its folding:
Blessed the hand
And the pen
That *his* hand was holding!"

1854

Klára Zách

(Sung by a bard in the fourteenth century)

The garden of the Queen
Blooms with a flower crown,
A rose of white, a rose of red,
A blonde girl, and a brown.

"My sister and my Queen,
In heaven's name I pray:
That rose, that red rose I have seen,
Would it were mine today!

"For ever after her I pine,
My heart beats till it ache;
Sure, of a thorn from that fair flower,
My death-wound I shall take!"

"Fie, brother Casimir,
That flower I'd never sell;
Go . . . I burn . . . where is thy shame? . . .
I fear this shall go ill!

"Needs must that I make haste
Unto the morning prayer;
If you be sick, lie down and rest
Upon my velvet chair."—

Then goes the Queen to church,
Then goes the Queen to prayer;
About her, lovely maiden flowers
Tend to her every care.

And well she now would pray,—
Yet cannot, in dismay;
Her rosary she left at home—
Who will go fetch it, say?

"Go, Klára, darling girl,
To me as daughter rare,
It lies upon my prayer-stool there,
Or on my long soft chair."

Now Klára searches long,
Finds nought, for all her pain;
My Lady Queen at church awaits
But she comes not again.

And Klára searches on,
An hour is gone, 'tis plain;
My Lady Queen waits in the church,
Waits, but she waits in vain.

The lost one comes no more
Among the virgins rare;
Better among the graveyard dead
Than where she spent that hour.

Better into the grave,
The black soil, make her way,
Than to the palace wide and great,
And to her father grey!

"Ho, daughter, daughter dear,
What ails thee, what ill cheer?
Come to my arms, my darling girl,
Tell me what grief breeds here."

"O father, father! No—
Ah, whither shall I go?
Let me in dust embrace your feet,—
To death then stamp me so . . . !"

And now the bells toll noon,
The day-feast comes full soon;

Then went the old Felicián
Before the King's high throne.

Before the King he went,
But not for dinner, sure;
For in his hand a dreadful sword
Of vengeance there he bore.

"Your death pays for my girl,
Elizabeth the Queen!"
With four fair fingers she has saved
Her life, by luck I ween.

"Your children for my child:
Lajos and Endre, die!"
Gyulafi runs upon the blade,
By luck, perhaps, ween I.

"Quick, run, go catch the churl . . .
My sons, Cselényi, run . . . !"
Felicián by the King's tall thanes
Is instantly cut down.—

"Thy fingers run with blood,
But will not bleed in vain:
What do you wish, my royal wife,
In payment for your pain?"

"For my first finger, lord,
His lovely virgin girl;
And for my thumb, his boy to death
In agony let hurl;

"And for the other two,
Daughter and son-in-law;
And for my red blood, into death
All of his kin let draw!"

Ill times indeed have come,
Ill stars above have we;
God save from such disaster, pray,
Our dear land, Hungary!

1855

The Bards of Wales

King Edward sits his palfrey grey,
Looks on his conquests' pales:
Let's see, says he, what worth to me
Is this domain of Wales?

What rivers flow, what harvests grow,
What meads for grazing good?
Is it well fed and waterèd
With rebel patriot blood?

Churls of this land, given by the hand
Of God into my care,
The folk, how do they love the yoke
They make their cattle bear?

No diamond fairer, gracious King,
Stands in your crown than Wales:
Land, river, grazing, all are there,
Mountains and fertile vales.

The folk indeed enjoy the yoke
God set upon them, Sire!
Their huts are dumb, as is the tomb
Upon the graveyard's mire.

And Edward walks his horse so pale
Amid his conquests bare:
All that remains are dumb domains
And silence everywhere.

Montgomery's that castle's name
Where the King lodged that night;
Montgomery, the castle's lord
Feasts him with all delight.

Fish, flesh, and fowl, and all things well
Fit for the flesh's gust,
A hundred servants, what a rout
To task the eyes' small lust;

And all that this fair isle might grow
To feed the belly's glee
And all the wines of foreign vines
Conveyed across the sea.

Gentles, gentles! is there not one
That clinks his glass to me?
Gentles, gentles! . . . you dogs of Wales!
May Edward's health not be?

Fish, flesh, and fowl, all under sky
Pleasing and sweet I see;
But yet methinks the devil slinks
In these lords' courtesy.

Gentles, gentles! you wretched dogs!
Who'll sing King Edward's tales?
Where is the guest who'll toast my geste—
Bring forth the bard of Wales!

Each in his neighbor's face now looks,
The many knights of Wales;
There upon every Welsh guest's face
A fearlike anger pales.

Words torn within, voice caught within,
Breath breaks and is drawn hard;
But now, above, a lone white dove,
Rises an old grey bard.

Here is, O King, one who will sing
Your deeds, says the old man;

The clash of battle, the death-rattle
Cry from the harp-string's pain.

"With clash of battle, with death-rattle,
Sun sets in its pool of blood,
The carrion-beast smells out the feast
Where you, King, spread the food!

"Our heaped-up dead, a cross of red,
The thousands that you slew:
The simplest churl that works the soil
Weeps at the scathe you do!"

The stake! Away! and no delay—
Edward commands the guard—
Ha! Here, a softer song we'll hear;
Up steps now a young bard.

"Ah! softly plays the evening breeze
That blows on Milford haven;
The maiden's keen, the widow's pain
Sigh in that wind of heaven.

Virgin, do not give birth to slaves!
Mother, do not give suck! . . ."
The King waves him away. He joins
The other at the stake.

A third, unbid and unafraid,
Yet comes before the King;
His harp speaks then as men speak men,
This Spell begins to sing:

"The good men all in battle fell—
Hear, Edward, what this tells:
Seek one who'd blaze your name with praise:
Lives not such bard of Wales."

His memory wrings the harp-strings still—
"Hear, Edward, what this tells:
Curse on your head is every song
Sung by a bard of Wales."

"This let us see!" The King commands
A deed at which hell pales:
"Burn at the stake all those who take
The proud name, bard of Wales!"

His servants ride out far and wide,
Gallop with his decree:
Thus was proclaimed that day the famed
Feast of Montgomery—

And Edward, King, rides a pale horse,
Gallops through hills and dales,
About him burns the earth's externes,
The fair domain of Wales.

Five hundred, truly, singing went
Into the grave of flame:
But no Welsh bard would sing this word:
"Long live King Edward's name!"

Holla! what clamor? . . . what night song
In London's streets then rang?
"If any voice disturb my rest,
The Lord Mayor shall hang!"

Silence stands dumb; no whisper heard,
Not even a fly's wing;
He risks his head whose word be said
That irks the sleepless King!

"Holla! bring music, pipe, and drum,
Let trumpets blast their scales!

The curses sear within my ear
Of that damned feast of Wales . . ."

But rising over scream of pipe,
The blare of bugle, drum,
Five hundred strong sing out their song
Of blood and martyrdom.*

1857

*While history is doubtful about the matter, legend strongly suggests that Edward, the English king, had five hundred Welsh poets executed after his conquest of the province of Wales, that they might not render their sons desirous to shake off the English yoke by singing the lays of their heroic past.—J.A.

The Ordeal of the Bier

In Radvány's dark forest they found him,
Bárczi Benő with a blade in his heart;
Long and keen was the dagger that downed him,
"Proof before God of the murderer's art:
Guilty the hand that has slain his young heart."

Him to the castle his father bids carry,
Set they him down in the chill of the tower;
Laying-out, washing—no rites customary;
He in his blood shall lie hour after hour,
Day after day on a crude makeshift bier.

Four halberdiers he charges to keep him
"No soul through this door shall enter or leave! . . ."
"Might not his mother, fair sister, come weep him?"—
"Back!" says the father, "however they grieve,
Woe to the guard that lets come without leave!"

Sobbing and softness of womanly grieving,
Muffled and hidden, from hall to long hall.—
Those *his* eye notes, in his hawk-like conceiving
Suspect, he calls to their trial by his seal:
"If the wounds bleed, that man's guilt they reveal."

Black is the cloth that beshrouds the great mansion,
Darkness at noon where the sun does not shine:
Sergeant at corpse-side stands at attention,
Priest in canonicals, cross, candles nine:
Flickering wax-light yellows his shrine.

"Let his foes come, if any there happen!"
In order they come, whom the father has named;
Vain! for the wound of the corpse will not open,

This one or that one may stand unashamed;
"Neither this one . . . nor that one . . . for murder be blamed."

"Then who? . . ." startles Bárczi, in dark desolation,
"This ancient blood unavenged shall not be;
Murderer, hither! . . . come face accusation,
Charged though *my* heart be with this felony:
Everyone living is suspect, to me!

"Let then be brought the young friends of his banner!"
Heroes well many in order march in,
Grieve that he died not in battle with honor,
Caked with his blood their beloved paladin.
Yet no red flows on the white of his skin.

"Let the court enter! the great and the lesser . . . !
Come, all the people that live in the town!"
Not a man leaves him unwept by his blesser,
Weeping their young lord so swiftly struck down.
Still, though, the wound remains clotted and brown.

"His mother, his sister!" and now for her brother
Outside is heard the high scream of her woe;
Cooing and cradling, on her son falls the mother,
Unmoved, the corpse will not open and flow:
Yet the cracked foulness no signal will show.

"Let come at last his beautiful lover,
Abigél Kund, promised secret his bride!"
She comes—and her eyes flash, are glued to the *dagger*;
Face turned to stone, feet rooted in stride.—
Red from the wound spouts the bubbling tide.

Not a tear rolls; and her grief makes no murmur,
Only she claws at the nest of the brain—
Dreadful the darting that pierces its armor! . . .

Shock to the heart freezes every vein:
"Daughter, you murdered the young chatelain!"

Twice this is said—she's struck dumb, in disorder—
Finally yields to her liege's demands:
"Bárczi Benö, no, I did not murder,
Witness the sky and its heavenly bands!
Ah, but this *dagger*—I placed in his hands!"

"He had my hand in true love—would he knew it—
There was no dam between him and my breast;
But with *hot words* he still urged me to '*do it*';
If not, he would kill himself. Lightly, in jest,
I gave him the dagger, and said: 'Be my guest.'"

And wildly she tears out the dirk from his body,
Eyes like a stranger's, flaming and fey;
Laughing and crying she flashes it, bloody,
And with a falcon-scream she runs away.
No hand dares touch her nor force her to stay.

Down the street headlong she runs through the city,
Shamed not to dance nor to sing on the way;
Merry the tune: "Once a girl who was pretty
Thought it fine sport with a young lad to play,
Just like the cat with a mouse for its prey!"

1877

Civilization

Formerly in war no moral
Laws existed to be broken:
From the weaker one the stronger
Took whatever could be taken.

Now it's changed. The world's directed
By a meeting or a treaty:
Still the stronger wreaks his mischief—
Justified by a committee.

1877

Red Rébék

"O'er the narrow footbridge scuttled
Red Rébék, then off she flew—"*
In a poplar tree she settled,
Preened herself as corbies do.
He to whom she croaks her "caw!"
Harm and scathe shall suffer sore,
'Roint thee, daw!

She it was who in black water
Boiled poor Dani Pörge's shoe,
Till he married Shinko's daughter,
Tera, girl more light than true.
Doubtless now he rues it sore,
Minds the cawing evermore,
'Roint thee, daw!

Now when Dani bumps that gipsy,
Pardon asks he not, and still
In the house a-catching, trips he
Ups-a-daisy, nose to sill.
Secretly she comes indoor,
"What a waste!" sighs evermore;
'Roint thee, daw!

Fancy wife, as if unheeding
Honeyed words, makes this reply:
"Make no wrangles in our wedding,
For no fickle wench am I!"
Auntie Rebi sighs the more:
What a pity! Caw, caw, caw!
'Roint thee, daw!

Next she comes and brings white money,
Kerchief red and gauds of art:
"Here, my daughter! Sweet as honey,

Let this good wine staunch thy heart:
Woe if beauty may not soar!"
"Let the bailiff in the door."
'Roint thee, daw!

Griefs enough and quarrels growing
Now at home make all things ill;
But the neighbors are unknowing:
Dani Pörge bears it still.
Cradle soon rocks on the floor:
Crow outside sings: caw-haw-haw!
'Roint thee, daw!

"Woman, devil! (Where's my musket?)
Take your father home this brat,
And this crow a picnic basket
For your journey I will shoot."
Now no more the crow sings: caw!
All her words stick in her craw:
"'Roint thee, daw!"

In the town the word speeds burning:
"Is it true what we've heard said?
Dani shot a *crow* this morning
But *Aunt Rebi* fell down dead!"
Rebi's soul grieves not a straw:
As a crow, returns to caw.
'Roint thee, daw!

Now for murder he is wanted:
Now what can poor Dani do?
Fugitive, he sets off, hunted,
On the footbridge sets his shoe,
Meets the bailiff of the law,
Crow is screeching: caw, caw, caw!
'Roint thee, daw!

Narrow is the bridge's footing,
Not enough for two, we deem;
Dani yields not; an upsetting,
And a great splash in the stream.
Deep it is, with spate and thaw.
Crow sees everything, says: caw!
'Roint thee, daw!

At a rustling leaf he'll shiver,
Life's a torment, on the run;
"Stranger, there, stand and deliver!"
Says above a loaded gun.
Crow is with him evermore:
"You'll get caught, my fine outlaw!"
"'Roint thee, daw!"

"Crows and ravens, lunch is ready.
Many though you are, you see
There's enough for everybody,
But the eyes—leave them for me."
Black as beetles though they are,
"Pity!" woman cries in awe,
"'Roint thee, daw!"

O'er the bridge with raven feather
Red Rébék still cawing flies;
From one corbie to another
Endlessly her soul it hies;
He to whom she croaks her "caw!"
Harm and scathe shall suffer sore,
'Roint thee, daw!

1877

*These two lines are fragments of a folk legend.—J.A.

My Complaints . . .

My complaints these days are legion:
Old catarrh, asphyxiation,
Crippling nervous purgatory,
Seeing, hearing, fragmentary,
And, impertinent, this glory.

1877–1878

SÁNDOR PETŐFI (1823–1849)

Prophecy

"Each night our dreams, you told me, Mother,
Are painted by a heavenly hand;
And every dream's a window, letting
Our eyes behold the future-land.

"Mother, I dreamed a dream; now could you
Untangle what it means for me?
I sprouted wings, and soared the heavens,
The bright air of eternity."

"My son, my soul's own sweetest day-star,
Sunlight to me! rejoice, I deem
God will stretch out your happy lifetime;
This is the secret of your dream."—

And the child grew, his youth enkindled
Into bright flame on his warm breast,
And song became his sovereign solace
When his hot blood boiled stormiest.

And now the youth's hand grasps the lyre-stem,
And gives his heart's-fire to the lyre,
And on the wings of song these flame-birds
Of feeling life fly everywhere.

The magic song flew up to heaven
And brought back down the star of fame,
And wove upon the poet's forehead
A coronal of gentle flame.

But the song's honey is a poison;
And what the poet gives the lyre
Must be his poor heart's every blossom,
Day by dear day fed to the fire.

To hell transforms the flame of feeling,
And he becomes the great pyre's prey;
Only a slim branch of the life-tree
Sustains his life's uncertain day.

And now he lies upon his deathbed,
The child of grief and agony,
And hears the sad lips of his mother
Murmuring in her misery:

"Death, tear him not from my embracing,
Let not the boy untimely die;
Long life was promised him by heaven . . .
Or are our dreams, too . . . all a lie?"

"Mother, the dreams are not untruthful;
Though in a shroud my dust may lie:
The great name of your son the poet
Lives on forever in the sky."

1843

I Would Be a Tree . . .

I would be a tree, were you the blossom,
If you were the dew, I'd be the bloom;
I would be the dew, were you the sunray . . .
So our two souls might as one relume.

If, my girl, you are the vault of heaven,
Then I would I might become a star.
If, my love, you're Hell, then (to be with you)
Let me be damned, as ruined spirits are.

1845

One Thought Troubles Me

One thought alone can strike dismay:
To pass pillowed in bed away!
To wither slowly like a fading flower,
Gnawed by the secret worm from hour to hour,
To shrivel like a candle in the gloom
That gathers slowly in an empty room.
O no such death, such cowardice,
God grant me no such death as this!
Let me be as the tree by lightning blasted,
Or by the storm uprooted and dismasted,
Let me be as the crag that battering thunder
Hurls from the heights into the depths asunder . . .
Then when all nations sick with thrall,
Faces aglow, in fields walk tall,
When they unfurl their banners crimson,
Writ with these sacred words, this holy ensign:
"World Liberation!"
And every nation
Clangs it and clangs it out from east to west,
While tyranny still threatens manifest:
That field of strife
Shall end my life:
Then from my heart shall sweetly flow the blood of youth,
And if my lips should echo then those words of truth,
Let them be drowned with the metallic clangor,
The cannon's crash, the trumpets' cry of anger;
Across my corse
The snorting horse
In squadrons gallop to their hard-won victory
And leave me trampled by the charging cavalry.—
There let them gather up my scattered bones
And with a sad, slow music's solemn tones
Let them observe the day of burial,

And under banners veiled in funeral
Devote their heroes to a common grave
Who died, world liberty, thy name to save!

1846

My Songs

Sunk in reverie I sometimes wonder
What those thoughts are, that my mind dreams under;
Up I fly, beneath me spreads the nation
Till I scan the whole world of creation;
Thence come songs whose fruit-time will inherit
All the moonrays of my dreaming spirit.

Better, perhaps, make future resolutions,
Than to live your life in mere illusions;
Maybe I should strive . . . ah, why this striving?
God is good and cares for my surviving.
Thence come songs whose fruit-time will inherit
Butterflies from my light-hearted spirit.

Lost in a love-tryst's ardent attentions,
Deeper I inter my apprehensions,
In my lovely mistress' eyes I'm gazing
As a star into the still sea's dazing;
Thence come songs whose fruit-time will inherit
Wild white roses from my amorous spirit.

Does she love me? joy turns me to drinking;
Loves me not? drink drowns all bitter thinking;
Where there is a glass and wine within it,
Pied delights rise fresh in every minute;
Thence come songs whose fruit-time will inherit
Rainbows from my mad and drunken spirit.

But, alas, the glass from which I'm drinking
Echoes the sound of nations' shackles clinking,
And the hand that holds the glass, so merry,
Mourns to be bound by freedom's adversary:
Thence come songs whose fruit-time will inherit
Darkened rainclouds from my grieving spirit.

How much more will the enslaved still bear it?
Why not break the chain, from free wrists tear it?
Must we then await, begging God's pity,
Rust to chew the shackles from the city?
Thence come songs whose fruit-time will inherit
All the lightnings of my wrathful spirit!

1846

September Ending

Still bloom in the valley the gardens of flowers,
The poplar's still greening by windows ajar,
But see how the winter-world lowers and lowers,
Already there's snow on the mountains afar.
Still young in my heart is the blazing-rayed summer,
There all of the springtime still blossoms so fair;
But see how my dark head is touched with a glimmer
Of wintery hoarfrost bethreading my hair.

As flowers must wither, so life must be fleeting . . .
So come, my betrothed, to my arms and my breast!
Shall you, whose sweet head on my heart hears its beating,
Tomorrow fall down on the grave where I rest?
If I should die first, O say, would you cover
My corpse with a pall, would you weep and exclaim?
And could a young swain, then, become your new lover,
And make you for his sake relinquish my name?

If ever you cast off the veil of the widow,
Yet hang it, dark banner, upon my gravestone,
And up from the grave-world shall rise my poor shadow
And take it at midnight, and fall back alone,
And use it to wipe off the tears I'd be shedding
For her who forsook her admirer and friend;
To dress the heart's wounds and to bind up its bleeding,
That, though in the grave, loves you yet without end!

1847

Song of the Nation

Magyars, rise, the nation bids you,
Now or never, when she needs you!
Liberty or base subjection,
Choose: that is the only question!—
To the God of Hungary
Let us swear,
Let us swear, we shall be captives
Nevermore!

Captive was our bleeding nation,
Cursed that ancient generation,
Who in freedom lived and perished
Slave soil should not hold uncherished:
To the God of Hungary
Let us swear,
Let us swear, we shall be captives
Nevermore!

Vagabond and faithless scoffer,
Who his death would fear to offer,
Who his ragged life holds finer
Than his homeland's wounded honor:
To the God of Hungary
Let us swear,
Let us swear, we shall be captives
Nevermore!

Brighter far is sword than fetter,
Fits a hero's arm far better;
Chains are all the grace we carry!
Come to us, old sword of glory!
To the God of Hungary
Let us swear,
Let us swear, we shall be captives
Nevermore!

Hungary, that name of beauty,
Ancient word for fame and duty,
We shall cleanse of her dishonor
Smeared by centuries upon her:
To the God of Hungary
Let us swear,
Let us swear, we shall be captives
Nevermore!

Where our graves are gently mounded
Grandchildren shall fall dumbfounded,
Whisper in that hallowed air
All our names in solemn prayer:
To the God of Hungary
Let us swear,
Let us swear, we shall be captives
Nevermore!

1848

Monstrous Days

Monstrous days, monstrous days!
Monstrousness waxing in its ways.
Has Heaven, in wrath,
Taken an oath
To crush the Magyar nation?
Our every limb's a bleeding gash,
Small wonder, when against us flash
The swords of half creation.

And now before us looms up War,
And scarcely less, but sad the more,
What drives us hence:
Grim Pestilence.
O Homeland, how you must writhe
Under the curse of God, while still
Upon your marches reaps at will
Fleshless Death's two-handed scythe.

And shall we all be lost? Or still
Someone survive our wreck who will
Write down in rhymes
These wild black times,
Giving witness as is fit?
And if one such remains, how shall
He rightly mourn our funeral,
That the world may know of it?

And if he truly testify,
To all that we have lived through, why
Should one who heard
Believe his word
Of so much grief and sorrow?—
And not take all this tale in doubt,

As what a mad brain monsters out
Upon that distant morrow?

1849

JÁNOS VAJDA (1827–1897)

Twenty Years Later

Like snow on Mont Blanc's distant crest,
That neither sun nor wind may harm,
My unvexed heart now lies at rest,
Inflamed by no new passion's charm.

Round me a myriad stars contend
Which casts the most flirtatious glow,
And on my head their bright rays bend,
Yet never do I melt or flow.

But sometimes on a silent night,
In lonely dreamings, half-awake,
Your swanlike image floats, so white,
On vanished youth's enchanted lake.

And then my heart flares up again,
As after a long winter's night
Mont Blanc's eternal snowfields, when
The rising sun turns them to light . . .

1876

JÓZSEF KISS (1843–1921)

Against the Tide*

White cumulus above the night—
Does God keep watch, or is there none?
Don't ask me—for I do not know,
But go to sleep, my little one!
That monster from grim centuries
Walks the Earth's wheel in unchecked ease,
The light of burning stakes, its eyes.
It could knock here before sunrise . . .
—But go to sleep, my little one!

From land to land it walks about,
A plague—disasters where it's gone;
All mercy dies upon its trail,
And Mind's great rights are overrun.
Madness makes riot everywhere,
All are obsessed, the foul and fair,
And those it takes, it eats, insane,
Until their names alone remain . . .
—But go to sleep, my little one!

The ancient charge won't go away;
Your father drinks warm blood, they'll say,
And you too, when you're fully grown,
Will drink blood as your father's done!
White cumulus above the night—
Does God keep watch, or is there none?
Torment if none; or God's at fault.
Either would crush me with its weight!
—But go to sleep, my little one!

The slander's easy, that we fail
To love this country where we dwell;

Birds love their nests, the beasts their lairs,
But you and I, we never shall!
The burned mark of the galley-slave
The jailer brands upon his brow
Is not so shameful as this slur
That lurks in every corner now . . .
—But go to sleep, my little one!

If you defend—then you offend;
If you are silent—cowardice!
If you cry out—you're sensitive;
Even a sigh draws prejudice!
The heart beats to a common law,
The blood pumps round, the brain conceives,
There's no exception, only one,
That's you, my child, my darling son! . . .
—So go to sleep, my little one!

Be dim, you lovely shining stars:
My little boy's sweet closing eyes!—
Why twinkle in such nights as ours?
The day that starlight testifies
Against me too, you'll realize
In burning tears and fruitless cries
What you inherit as my son,
My beautiful, my little one!

1882

*A response to the infamous anti-Semitic blood libel trial of 1882.

Oh Why So Late

Oh why so late, now autumn is unleaving,
Cranes are leaving, why did we delay?
Why not in the sweet time of the rose-blooming
Sacred gloaming of the break of day?

Why could we not, sweet couple, listen hidden
To the lark unbidden, you and I?
Why did we not in that hour drunk with yearning,
Young dreams burning, come together, why?

1884

JENŐ HELTAI (1871–1957)

Among My Songs

The part that one might call prevailing
Among my songs, madam, of late
—And why should I deny my failing—
Were writ for you, my little Kate.

That moiety, deemed so prevailing,
Among those little songs of late,
You found, madam, less than appealing;
Indeed you loathed them, little Kate.

I "thou"'d you, true, in ways revealing
Motives deemed inappropriate,
"You" surely the more proper styling
When one addresses little Kate.

But that part one might deem prevailing
Among those songs you execrate
Were writ with all my heart's true feeling
Straight to your heart, my little Kate.

So if, from all your cold reviling,
Which one might malheureusely call your hate,
I die in grief of such misdealing,
You are to blame, my little Kate.

Then blame yourself, my little Kate,
If nought remains of me but ailing
Songs you did not appreciate
(The ones that one might call prevailing).

1884

ENDRE ADY (1877–1919)

"I Am the Son of Gog and Magog . . ."

(Untitled epigraph to a new collection of poetry)

I am the son of Gog and Magog*;
In vain I beat at the fortifications,
And I ask you: is it forbidden to cry out
Under the ramparts of the Carpathians?

To the famed pass of Verecke** I came,
The bawling hornblast of the old Magyar tunes in my ears,
Can I smash through at Dévény***
With the new songs of the new years?

Go ahead, pour hot lead in my ears,
I'd be the new Vazúl,† a criminal of song.
Better not let me hear the new songs of life!
Yes, stamp me down, crush me in my harangue.

But till then, shrieking in pain, hoping for nothing,
Still the song flies on, on its own bright pinion,
And cursed by the blood-elders of Pusztaszer†† a hundred times over,
It's still victorious, it's still new, it's still Hungarian.

1905

---

*Gog and Magog are ancient names in the Book of Genesis. Ady poetically claims them as the Hungarians' Central Asian origins.

**The easternmost mountain pass of Hungary.

***The westernmost mountain pass.

†Vazúl, seeking to preserve the old Magyar traditions, was caught in his attempt to assassinate his cousin King Stephen, the first Christian king of Hungary (later canonized as a martyr). Vazúl's punishment was having molten lead poured in his eyes and ears.

††Pusztaszer is the name of a location in Hungary where, according to chroniclers, seven Magyar tribal chiefs decided to unite and entered a blood compact with one another.

Hawk-Mating on the Forest Floor

Hellbent for Autumn, screeching, crying,
Off we went in chase of each other,
Two hawks, droop-winged, all a-flutter.

Summer is rife with these young robbers.
Fresh and frenzied, our pinions rattle,
Kissing rages in loving battle.

Fleeing Summer we fly our pursuing;
Somewhere in Autumn we settle together,
Love shaking each disheveled feather.

This is to be our final mating;
Tearing each other's flesh we glitter,
Fall now, spent, in Autumn leaf-litter.

1905

The Poet of the Eastern Plains

Large-eyed and Kunish, a mooning boy,
Aching, aching with voiceless yearnings,
Herdsman he was, of the famed plainlands,
Hortobagy's taciturn mornings.

Nightfall-skies and mirage-horizons
Seized his soul a hundred times over,
But every flower his heart would blossom
The herdfolk grazed off like the clover.

Mind full of a thousand miracles,
Dreams of death, of wine, of Woman,
Anywhere else he'd have been a poet,
Sacred, the prophet of the human.

Seeing his mates in their oafish long johns,
Grazing with beasts on grass and thistle,
Soon he learned to bury his singing,
Knew no more than to curse and whistle.

1905

On New Waters I Walk

Fear not, my ship, for you carry Tomorrow,
The drunken oarsman they jeer at, the hero.
Fly, my brave ship,
Fear not, my ship, for you carry Tomorrow.

Ever soaring, soaring, forever soaring
New Waters, huge Waters, virginal, roaring,
Fly, my brave ship,
Ever soaring, soaring, forever soaring.

What need have I of last season's dreamed dreamings?
New waters I walk, new pains, secrets, yearnings.
Fly, my brave ship,
What need have I of last season's dreamed dreamings?

I won't play fiddle for the grey ones' capers
In the holy ghost's or the taproom's vapors;
Fly, my brave ship,
I won't play fiddle for the grey ones' capers.

1905

Autumn Came to Paris

Autumn dropped in to Paris yesterday,
Slipped along Saint-Michel so quietly
—Though it was dog days under summer boughs—
And there it met with me.

Strolling toward the Seine I felt my soul
Kindling with newborn songs in fiery breath;
Smoky, strange ones, purple, melancholy,
Each one about my death.

Autumn caught up with me and whispered something,
Saint-Michel quivered with it, and the leaves—
Swish-swish!—flew helter-skelter on the street
In pranks the Fall wind weaves.

A moment only: summer scarcely flinched;
Autumn fled Paris laughing in the breeze;
It came, and only I knew that it came,
Under the moaning trees.

1906

Legend of Saint Margaret

One night of ancient tales the Rabbit Island
Confessed to me its secret. This was it:
Her royal father cast into a cloister
The legendary maid, white Margaret.

A girl of dreams she was: a scream unuttered.
One uncouth word could lay her in a swoon.
This was a court where brutish shaggy warriors
Rumbled and tossed their beards midnight and noon.

Long years she waited for her western lover,
Not some mustached and hirsute warlord boor.
A soft boy he, melodious, delicate,
A girlish, vague, and tearful troubadour.

Long time she waited, and her heart stood spellbound.
The castle buzzed, and boastful Huns rode in
From battle on their whinnying Turkish horses.
He never came, her dream-quiet paladin.

He never walked here in the Danube-lands,
That lad of songs and kisses soft and shy;
To Jesus then they offered Margaret,
And on the Isle of Rabbits she would die.

1906

Confessions of the Danube

Our Danube, this old fox, I've just found out,
Hides secrets that in all the ages gone
Were never dreamed of or imagined
Since the first cave-fires began to burn
By Europe in its oblivion.

I stole those secrets from old Ister, I,
Secrets the dark Danube used to bear.
Sly the old scoundrel is on Magyar soil,
He's seen the grimmest marvels happen there.
But he got gossipy then, I swear.

I don't even know just when he confessed:
It was spring; he was drunken-silly.
He danced, sang, whooped, told boozy anecdotes,
Whistled rude ballads in the valley,
Sneered at Budapest satirically.

Perhaps it was on famed St. Margaret's Isle
He buttonholed me, in fuddled spate.
Even now my heart thrashes out of step,
For heigh-ho, this song comes too late.
Is it true, Ister, old reprobate?

But Danube now got grand and serious.
His wild spring mood cooled upon his lips.
Eyes hardly daring to look into mine,
He seemed some kind of genius in his cups;
I questioned him, pressed him, pulled out the stops.

"So, old sot, you've seen a miracle
Or two, in the years you've washed these shores
With the pale ghastly shades of your waters,
Night of our most ancient ancestors.
Confess, old blackguard: open up your doors.

"Was the world always so ill-fated here?
Primal vice, lukewarm left-handed sin,
Shivering, struggle, tears, disastrous drought?
On Danube's marches have there never been
Folk happy, laughing, strong, genuine?"

Softly murmuring old Danube began
The story. Indeed, that we are cursed,
As many of us guessed, it's all too true:
No happy folk dwelt here from the first
Dark spring through which the ancient river burst.

The Danube's banks are a sad lightning rod
For half-people, semi-nationlets,
Created for a pillory of shame.
Where wings are clipped, where the tired sun sets
Into a dusk of deathly silhouettes.

"It was ordained so, it will never change,"
Muttered old Danube's chilly white foam.
And through those wretched little countries stretched
That old good-for-nothing, quite at home.
And laughed, and ran away into the gloam.

1907

From the Stream to the Ocean

The stream's a big ditch, strange and sleepy:
Weed, water, bullrush, mud, and motion.
But Kraszna, Szamos, Tisza, Danube
Bear off its bubbles to the ocean.

If Scythian heights should overhang me,
If curses block my blood and passion,
If moles in thousands dam my courses,
Yet still I'll reach that distant ocean.

I want it, that dark gloomy courage,
Want it, world's miracle and mission,
That one can start out from a streamlet
And flow to the great holy ocean.

1907

And I Am Not a Hungarian?

Ancient Dawn-lands dreamed him such
As I am.
Heroic, cloudy, proud, inordinate,
Cruel, but one who'll bleed to death
For no more than a thought.
Ancient Dawn-lands dreamed him such,
He the courageous, the new, the wild,
Noble, forever the great child,
Heartbreaking, disconsolate,
The thirsty, sun-souled errant knight,
Hurt masterpiece of some poor luckless god,
Wounded and incomplete,
Hungarian, son of the Sun.
(And to the sleepy one, the dirty one,
The crippled one, the fancy one,
The one who's half-alive, the foaming one,
The super-Magyar one, fog-eating one,
The Swabian turned Hungarian,
I am not a Hungarian?)

1907

The Voiceless Birds

There they fly by every noonday,
Summer noonday,
In the sizzling light-beams of the brilliant Sun:
Golden-feathered, golden-ruffled,
One by one.

Treasure-birds, magical griffins,
Voiceless griffins,
Vultures, staring at the Sun and cursed with spells.
Diamond on haughty diamond
Are their skulls.

Soundless in their august silence,
Tearful silence.
If they were to cry out, they would fall away,
Like the grey-predestined sparrows,
Turn to grey.

Still they fly by every noonday,
Summer noonday,
Glittering in their dark pride beneath the sun:
Golden-feathered, golden-ruffled,
One by one.

1907

On Elijah's Wain

The Lord, as Elijah, takes all those,
The ones he loves and smites with pains:
He gives them their swift and flaming hearts,
And those, then, are the fiery wains.

The Elijah-folk rush at the Sky,
To halt at eternal winter's reign,
On Himalaya's ice-bitten crests
Groans on in clouds of dust their wain.

Grief-homeless still, between Earth and Sky,
Driven by the winds of Fate they strain:
Toward that beautiful, baleful chill
Gallops Elijah's fiery wain.

Their hearts are burning, their brains are ice,
The Earth laughs at their hope and trust:
But on their ice-road the ruthful Sun
Sprinkles a frigid diamond-dust.

1908

Thank You, Thank You, Thank You

Dazzling in my ears is the roar of the sun,
Sweet in my mouth the savor of your name,
Loud in my eyes your holy thunder,
Lord of light, lord of sweetness, lord of wonder:
Last night my soiled soul confessed everything—
You were always there, everything in everything,
There in my joyful following of the scent,
There in the tender rush of lovemaking,
There in my watchings, my sharp sad intent:
And now thank you for simply being there,
There where instinct said my life must be,
Where the altars fall down and rise again.
I thank you for the bed made up for me,
Thank you for that first great sob of pain,
Thank you for my mother's broken heart,
Thank you for my youth and for my sin,
Thank you for faith, thank you for doubt,
Thank you for the kiss, and for the sickness that came,
Thank you that I owe nobody anything,
Only you, to whom I owe everything.
Dazzling in my ears is the roar of the sun,
Sweet in my mouth the savor of your name,
Loud in my eyes your holy thunder,
Lord of light, lord of sweetness, lord of wonder.
My soul is light now that has confessed and seen
That you were the kiss, the anguish, the life-breath
And thank you at last that you shall be my death.

1911

The Abandoned Pirate Ships

Daybreak. And at last my ship is the real one:
I fly with it, mounded with morning flowers.
I don't recognize him, the old stout pirate;
I am become the golden boy of huzzahs, desires:
My joyous ship beflagged with a nuptial veil
Is a blue veil cut out of the skies.
The sun is laughing through my fire eyes:
No ship he's ever seen is such a miracle,
No sailor so sea-morning-like, so endawned.
Our desire gushes before us its own seas,
This very Ocean becomes my own.
And it rocks me in the rhythm of our arms,
And the superstitious foghorn blares its hymns,
And the bridge is singing kissing-melodies.
My mast the promise of victory,
Of that intoxicating virgin-given kiss;
And now it's the old pirate-ships that haunt me,
In which so long I had wandered plundering,
Yet Night's power was in vain to drive me—
It is not her lap to which I now have come—
Sunrise called me forth, sunrise.
And after all my new ship still came for me—
Oh past ships, what shadows you've become!
Oh past prey, how you've lost your savor!
I'm freer than any free man could be,
Though truly I am not all my own.
What past ship now could my eyes desire?
The hungry little green-flagged ship
Of agonized uncertain youth?
My storm-ship whereby I left behind
The shabby little poets' outdated songs?
Or perhaps the flag-waving, boring,
Hundred-skirted gross kiss-ship of my whoring?

Or the ugly pirate ship of fame,
Drunkenness, wisdom, and the praised name?
Alas, here's the girl upon my heart,
Here's my heart where I relive, rejoice in
The bright hours, the true life of the sea:
Proudly I carry now, now I have become Me,
Into these holy youth-storms of reality
What is the only embrace-worthy:
The ship of new Life, heavy with destiny.

1914

I Guard Your Eyes

With this now so ancient hand,
With these now so ancient eyes,
I am clasping your young hand,
I keep guard upon your eyes.

From the wreck of worlds I come,
Time-worn beast that seeks to hide,
Driven by fear-delirium,
And I cower by your side.

With this now so ancient hand,
With these now so ancient eyes,
I am clasping your young hand,
I keep guard upon your eyes.

I don't know how long I'm given
To be with you, whens and whys,
But I'm clasping your young hand
And keep guard upon your eyes.

1916

Memory of a Summer Night

Sky-borne, a crazy angel drummed
Warning to the somber earth:
More than a hundred boys unseamed,
More than a hundred stars eclipsed,
More than a hundred brides undiademed,
What a strange,
Strange summer night that seemed.
Our old beehive caught on fire,
Our most comely colt's leg broke,
And the dead walked, so I dreamed,
Burkus, our good dog, got lost,
Poor dumb Mary, who's our maid,
Ranting songs she sang and screamed;
What a strange,
Strange summer night that seemed.
All the nobodies got loud,
And the real men hid away,
Even the pickiest burglars climbed;
What a strange,
Strange summer night that seemed.
We all know how frail mankind is,
Can't repay the love it's given:
Still, it was odd how, all unframed,
The world turned upside down that night.
More mocking now the moon has never been:
Never so jeering, never so small,
So void of awe was Man as on that night.
What a strange,
Strange summer night that seemed.
Horror bent down over people's souls,
Sneering with pleasure, down it loomed,
Into each human being crept
The secret fate of his ancestors;

Into a monstrous, bloody wedding
Thought, our proud swain, lo and behold,
Went drunk, besotted, paralyzed,
A gawping nobody, unashamed.
What a strange,
Strange summer night that seemed.
I believed, at that time I believed
That a neglected god revived,
Rose into another life,
And bore me to the realms of death.
Yet see, I live and breathe here still,
He whom that night reconceived,
God-awaiting, I recall
That horrific night when all
The world itself was foundered quite:
What a strange,
Strange summer night that seemed.

1917

Behold, Love, These My Treasures

These jewels your love possesses,
Lazarous, pathetic nothingnesses,
See, they're the fate of truth and loyalty:
Behold my greying tresses.

I went not hither-thither;
Magyar pride was all my plume and feather,
Which I reaped in woe and woeful folly
And all that pain and bother.

And I was such a lover:
No god could have loved love more and braver
Than I, a child, in my imaginings;
See now my sores, blood, fever.

Had you not come, my waning
Voice might now have ceased from its complaining;
I would now be laid within my coffin
By mockers of life's meaning.

Look at me, love, and seeing,
Love me; I found you while I was fleeing;
And what joy survives the world's malignance
My heart stores in your being.

These jewels your love possesses,
Lazarous, pathetic nothingnesses,
Lie with yours, so rich and dark and youthful:
Behold my greying tresses.

1917

MARGIT KAFFKA (1880–1918)

Pagan Prayer

Great Gods! Enough, enough of silence!
This peace is strangling me,—it makes me ill.
Where's the storm-wind, for my defying laughter?
All's quiet here, all smiles, all imbecile.

However torn, upon the foam-flecked ocean,
Free sails fly yet so fair and joyfully!
Vile—that I must wait grounded, without motion,
Till spider-woven ivy climbs on me.

Great Gods! I pray you gather me together
All glittering and blood-bespattered days,—
Distil for me that one life from forever,
And set each fiery minute in a blaze!

Take back those dull years gravid with indifference:
Others can have them all, for all I care.
Give just one day!—but buried in mad blisses,
Or else a feast of lightnings be my share!

1902

Little Peter Walks

Two catfish-mouthed, silly, minikin booties,
Absurd and endearing, fit for a gnome,
Uncertain, hesitant—with a fairylike rustle
Just toddle across this decrepit old room.
—And now in my heart a playful mood wakens,
I'm spread with a rain of snowy-white flowers.—
Seeing him now I can't help it, my laughter
Bursts out aloud in sweet-feeling showers.
So across all these old things, these grey writings,
Run hundreds of light-rays in swift little shocks,
And I'd like to call out to them, one and another:
—Pit-pat! He's started. Petey-kin walks!

Still he holds tight to the leg of the table,
Opens his lips, turns so red! Like a brand
On fire with the human heroic fever,
This little rosebud has just learned to stand.
Now,—now! He sets off, leaves it behind him,
Such stumbles, meanders, in his first gallant cruise!
Pit-pat! Sometimes stopping, yet always persisting,
Heroic'ly patter the silly dwarf shoes.
He's close. Now he stretches both arms to his mother.
—"Just slowly, cleverly, Petey old chap!"
And hurrying now,—no time to fall headlong,
Leans forward—and suddenly he's in my lap.

The game pleases him. So let's play another.
Alongside the old easy chair I crouch down.
One big-long step, and big—soon he'll catch Mother,
But the poor thing collapses before he's begun.
His lips start to shake, he's thinking of crying,
Looks round, is somebody sorry for him?
He's thinking . . . then up he gets, and with a whimper,
Starts out afresh, now resolute, grim.

Pointing before him his pink little forefinger,
Pit-pat!—he sets forth across the great gap,
Softly, lisping, he cheers himself up with:
"Just slow-ly! clever-ly! Petey-old-chap!"

I gaze at him ceaselessly, eyes getting blurry,
A misty mirage comes down on my sight.
. . . The years disappear . . . I'm aging already . . .
And it seems I can hear the tread of strong footsteps,
And there at the door is a knightly young man,
—"It's you? What can I get for you? Cake? or coffee?"—
Pit-pat! an old woman, I walk round my son.
And while he regales me, laughingly, merrily,
With spoofs and surprises, this struggle, that scrap—
Trembling, frightened, I privately whisper:
Just slowly,
Just slowly, cleverly, Petey old chap.

1903

To Appear Before You

How soft, my tired woman's hand,
How soft it strokes, how gentle when it gives,
Opening, to that wherein it lives—
Through you I came to understand:
Blessings on you for giving me my hand!

My eyes, soever languid, thoughtful, sad,
(Amazing miracle!) beheld your fate
And knew it as a burning brand immaculate,
Star of Bethlehem, guide from paradise,
God bless me for the vision of my eyes!

I'm ugly, that's what I always thought,
Tuning tuned only for coarse desire,
To charm the heart I never might aspire.
—You loved me, charmed me with a caress
Into this soft evening loveliness.

So ugly was it, how I lived till now,
Mixed, wasteful, in half, torn agape! . . .
Now my past, too, has been set in shape
As now I tell the story of it all.—
Because you saw my fate: I found it beautiful.

The golden chalice of your faith
Brimfull you offered, holy, brave, and fine.
You gave me for to drink your love's grailwine,
And sainted me for all my days!
Beatified: raised high within your praise
Ever "appearing before you"; for these things,
O blessings, blessings, blessings, blessings!

1915

GYULA JUHÁSZ (1883–1937)

How It Was

Her blondness, how it was, I can't remember,
But I know the fields are blond with grain
When rich-eared wheat brings in the yellowing summer
And its blondness calls her back again.

How blue her eyes were, now I don't remember.
But when Fall unfolds the opening skies
The weary valedictions of September
Dream me to the color of her eyes.

How silk her voice was, too, I don't remember,
But in spring, when fields of grasses sigh,
Anna's voice, its intimate warm timbre,
Calls from a spring as distant as the sky.

1912

Profane Litany

Anna lost, gold mansion,
Precious miracle,
Ivory-encarven
Joyous citadel.

Anna lost, bright faerie,
Eden's sweet bouquet,
Whence fate's sword forever
Drove me once away.

Anna lost, high heaven,
Land beyond far Thule,
You of whom, so distant,
Thought can be so cruel!

All that might be treasured
I lay at your feet,
As before her mistress
Kneels the slave-girl sweet:

Ever, orphan-sculpture,
Stiff in your high throne,
As on Doric temples
Goddesses of stone!

1912

MIHÁLY BABITS (1883–1941)

Evening Questioning

On such an evening time, soft coverlet
of velvet black a giant nurse has set
and smoothly spread upon this cherished world
so carefully that every grass-stem pearled
stands up unruffled under this slow veil
and flower petals, wrinkleless, glow pale
and even the pied, fragile butterflies
lose no enamel from their rainbow wings,
and all the much-loved planet resting lies
under this light veil's velvet shadowings,
not feeling aught of weight or of oppression
but covered gently as a prized possession:
then wheresoever in the world you wander,
or in your sad brown room behind the glass,
or in a quiet café you watch and ponder
as one by one they light the sun-bright gas;
or tired out, with your dog upon a hill,
you see through branches the slack moon stand still;
or on the road, dusty and overdone,
your dozing cabbie sleepily drives on;
or on a ship's deck, dizzy with the heaving,
or in the thrumming carriage of a train,
or in a foreign city idly roving
you stop upon the corner of a lane
to watch, pleased, how the distant avenues
make double threads of lamp-flame, twos by twos;
or here, at Riva, in the water-city,
where the matte opal mirror splits the rays,
you, musing, cry for lost felicity,
seek back for memories of former days,
the ache of your lost youth, which like the embered

image of a magic lamp both is
and is not, ever warm and still remembered,
an unborn treasured burden, painful bliss;
your head may then, heavy with memories,
hang down toward the marble ground for this:
roaming amid such beauty and delight
you will, despite these gifts, in cowardice
think this: why all this beauty? in despite,
orphaned you will ask what is it all for?
why the silk waters, the pied marble floor?
why the soft evening, this winged coverlet?
why the dark branches, why the hill? and why
the seas wherein no seedsman sows? and why
the ditches, and the droughts, and in the sky
the clouds, those maiden-sad Danaïdes,
the burning stone of Sisyphus, the sun?
why the past times, why all those memories?
why the lamp-lightings, why the lazy moon?
why time, that ever seeks its end in vain?
or take the grass blade, tiny as a feather:
why does the grass grow, when it needs must wither?
why does it die, when it will grow again?

1909

Ode on Beauty

Music, madonna! What is it you hear,
what secret music through our air's clogged sea,
that every quiver of your measure here
should answer to its silent melody?
Even your pinkie's tiniest muscle, see,
moves not except to make the measure clear,
your step likewise, this dance, this revelry,
this floating visual music holds so dear
it tunes my stringed heart to the concord of its ear.

This is the spheres' music! World melody,
which takes your body for its instrument,
or was it nature's magics, drifting free
for eons about the starry firmament
that found your precious body excellent
to lens-like sheaf, collect the sun's gold rays,
a glass of precious water, opulent,
and pour that light out to the world's amaze:
to dwell in sight of you is a surpassing grace.

And should this dear flesh fall into the grave,
this precious lens be broken (mourn, O muse!
for all will crumble, all that nature gave
come to that last ditch and its final ooze,
the ripe fruit marred by winter's darkening bruise);
still what was beautiful, that ray so fair,
that *light-beam* shall the ether so infuse
that lost to human sight soever, there
the ray remains, a profit for the gods to share.

Happier mortals of another star
perhaps will catch that traveling music-light
and read, after some few millennia,
your body-poem's eternal wave-delight.

O may I hope with their hope, when your bright
ray only *then* blossoms in their strange skies,
passing from star to star across the night,
that from your body's holy vessel flies
like precious steam drifting out of a dish of sacrifice.

Your earthly monument may crack and cave,
and the earth too will crumble: mourn, O muse!
for all will crumble, all that nature gave
come to that last ditch and its final ooze;
The ray flies on in space-time's avenues.
Body and soul die: but it cannot die.
This treasure's one that all vast space may use,
and so from star to star it will still fly
into infinity, for the gods to profit by.

1909–1911

Love Poem

Lake of your eyes, dark grey, your face's deepest deeping,
under the snowscape of your brow, your snowbrow's sleeping,
I love them and I love how I forget the snow in summer's amazing
in your eyes' summer giddiness I sing the giddy flash of their blazing.

Bottomless lake of ore, ore-mirror, precious metal, fairytale magic-mine,
giddy in their flash, who knows how deep goes that shine?
Spirit ore-lake, the noblest innermost metalline
souls shine there in their profound glitter; but what kind of gold-steel-
   silver spirit glows so fine?

In your deep bright-metal grey lovely hued eyes, sweeting,
miraculous, glittering bells chime there silently, silently, fleeting
—so you can't hear it or see it yet there it's beating
only for him who loves you as much as I do, sweeting, sweeting.

1920

Evening Arrival

The greedy miles consume
this still and dark perfume,
dusk's soft and meadowy soul
into a distant gloom.
Now my car windows
are struck with sudden light,
street lamps in two bright rows
meet me from the night.

By now the darkness is
but a torn blanket;
only the burning sky
is with me yet;
my hiker's tired hands
let fall away
into the rushing street
silence's grass-sweet bouquet.

But the blazing lamps blare
their glaring elements
into my dazzled eyes
in clashing violence.
In the soft night, elsewhere,
there is a deathly silence;
here glitters electricity,
the city's brilliance.

Here, below, the city
flashing out its rays.
but above, the heavens'
hundred stars ablaze;
lamps, the earthly kingdom,
stars, the heavenly,

lamps, the now-becoming,
stars, eternity.

1923

Between Fall and Spring

Now autumn's wine-song echoes and is still.
Stifling and close the cellar's summer chill.
Now wind and water beat the naked vine.
Now gooseflesh pocks the clay-hill's pallid skin,
the earth is rotten, melts itself to mud,
as does the naked body of the dead.

It's evening, and the evenings of this season
hurry like thievish age in silent treason:
old age that creeps on tiptoe hour by hour,
then leaps, and suddenly we're in its power!
We can deceive ourselves no more; we cry
O grief that we must die, that we must die!

Fresh snow has fallen on the wretched soil,
as if its ugliness cried for a veil.
As is a new-made bed, the ground is white,
prepared for us and waiting for the night,
downy, soft, pillowed, immaculate:
and just like children who have stayed up late,

we mischievously walk upon our bed—
children who won't be tucked beneath the spread
and swaying balance on the coverlet
until their loving mother tires of it
and calls to them, "Get under now, bye-bye!"
O grief that we must die, that we must die!

The year like an hourglass turns, replaced,
the yore one's spent, the new shrinks through its waist;
and as the glass's used-up sand pours through,
the old year leaves its troubles to the new.
For so much work remains undone, unsaid!
And pleasure's tree is yet unharvested . . .

Our heart, impatient sentry, loathes delay;
it hastes its beat, relief is on the way.
A hundred drawers we open, nervously.
A farewell-tasting kiss thrills curiously.
Old joys cannot console, we gasp a sigh:
O grief that we must die, that we must die!

The snow is melting, spring waits eagerly.
What do I know, what do I want to be!
I am a feather, melting with the snow,
that sighs to tears and melts into a flow.
And when the birds return, the earth is sere,
and winter's name has passed on like the year.

Only my winter's not so quick to fly.
Only my death cannot contrive to die.
Whomever in my life I would set free,
that bird would never yet return to me.
My fallen leaves will not revivify:
O grief that we must die, that we must die!

So one by one my friends have left my side.
By those I helped I later was denied.
Those whom I loved in turn do not love me,
those whom I glittered for would bury me.
Whatever word my branch wrote in the dust
is swept away by spring mud and is lost.

The wine, last year's spent guest, dries uselessly,
to me even the spring's an enemy!
Only you cover me, womanly good,
as roses do the trellis' broken wood,
kissing my frightened eyes with lullaby . . .
O grief that we must die, that we must die!

1935

Saint Blaise-ing*

Graciously intercede for me, help me, Saint Blaise!
In my childhood two white candles
were laid on my frail neck in the form of a cross
and I peered between the candles
as a frightened deer watches between two branches.
Midwinter, on Blaise's name-day
my eye hung bemused and blinking on the old priest,
who offered up a prayer to you,
bending above me as I knelt at the altar
according to the gentle custom,
and mumbling in Latin, which neither he nor I
well understood. In spite of this
you listened to him and stood guard on my childish
life-breath against the throttling grippe,
the lizard, the flaming pit of the uvula,
all so that when I had grown up
I'd live ungratefully for half a century
without giving you the least thought.
Oh, don't mind my ugly thoughtlessness, protect me
now too, bishop of Sebasta!
That's how we live, you see, foolishly, childishly;
we run away and don't look back
on the world's buzzing highroad, let go of your hands
—you higher spirits!—but you just
smile and indulge our folly like clever adults
Not hurt when we disregard you
and then we run back to you in our necessity
as I do now before you, with
this trembling heart . . . smile at me now, blessed Saint Blaise!
who like a whimpering urchin
kneel here on the naïve stone of your simple altar—
smile at my folly, but just help!
For this cruel traitor, the crab, is just killing me,

it's got a choke-hold on my throat,
my windpipe's crushed, my wind is getting short, my lungs
gasp for their air, as a climber
crawls up a mountain under a heavy burden,
all out of breath, that's how I live,
panting and panting always. And the doctors' knives
are readying now to cut my
bad neck, which once I so willingly bent to you
between the cross of your candles
as if I had already foreknown it . . . Help, Blaise!
Because your saintly larynx too
was cut apart by knives, when the evil pagan
put you to death: you know it all!
You know the sharpness of the blade, the taste of blood,
the long tensedness of the minutes,
the cramps of the torn windpipe, and the struggle of
choking, and above all the dread.
Help! You've been through everything, you're over it all,
clever grown-up! You know it well,
just how much suffering humankind can bear, how much
God's goodness, even, finds too much,
and how much life is worth . . . and know this too, perhaps;
that death is not so big a thing.

June 1937

   *St. Blaise is the patron saint of cancer victims. The peculiar word-construction of the title is Babits's own.

The Prayer of Jonah

The words, unfaithful, will not serve my thought,
or like a flooding stream, irresolute,
I wander aimless bound to no sure shore
wearing the old vain words I wore before
as the wayward flood in its lostness bears
fenceposts signposts timber of dams and weirs.
Oh might the Master give my current's maze
a bed and channel, in unerring ways
to take it to the sea, and in good time
fit out my poems' margins with a rhyme
that's ready-made, His holy Bible be
upon my shelf my only prosody,
might, like His lazy servant Jonah, I,
hiding, or in the Fish, have taken my
descent into the living, deaf, and hot
abyss and dark of agony, but not
for three days, but three months, three years, an ill-
formed century, to find, before the still
blinder eternal Whale-mouth swallows me
and I am lost forever in that sea,
my old voice, and my words in good array,
flawless as He has whispered them, oh may
I speak with courage from my crippled throat
and not grow weary till the sun goes out
while heavenly or Ninevehan powers
still let me speak and shorten not my hours.

1939

DEZSŐ KOSZTOLÁNYI (1885–1936)

Autumn Breakfast

This is the gift that autumn brought. Cool fruits
on a glass plate. Heavy, dark-emerald
grapes, gigantic jasper-shining pears,
all of Fall's opulent and glowing jewels.
There on a berry scurries a water-drop,
rolls like a diamond down its bright plump flank.
This is pure splendor, cloudless, dispassionate,
perfection turning inward to itself.
Better to live, perhaps. But still, beyond,
the trees are beckoning with their golden hands.

1929

Ilona

Feather-light
Weaver-girl,
Moon and shine
Is your smile,
Sol and fa
Of your name:
Ilona,
Ilona.

Let my soul
Silently
Sing its song,
Lalala,
Lullaby,
Nurse your name,
Ilona,
Ilona.

As it were,
In my ear,
I can hear
Gentle gales,
Weiala,
Mermaid-song,
Swaying souls,
Ilona.

Muezzin
Drones the same
"La Illah
Il' Illah"
As I sing
In your name,

Ilona,
Ilona.

In the home
Of the light
Comes and goes
Light and night,
Retina,
Nebula,
Ilona,
Ilona.

Odds and ends
Of my dreams
Play the fool,
Ephemera
Of the soul
Touch the lyre,
Ilona,
Ilona.

O the charm
Of the "I,"
Melody
Of the "L,"
Oh and Ah
Of the old
Balladry,
Ilona.

Full of "L,"
Full of "I,"
Full of "O,"
Full of "Ah,"
Full of milk,

Full of joy,
Full of woe,
Ilona.

And I saw
Colors there,
Brilliant-pale,
Silica,
Purple-jale,
Aniline,
Viola,
Ilona.

Festival,
Agony,
Gall and man-
Dragora,
Balsamine,
Heavenly
Lanolin,
Ilona.

Floating life's
Gentle dawn,
Evening's last
Soft huzzah,
Never lost,
Never gone,
Ilona,
Ilona.

Langorous
Angels sigh;
Thus they cry
In their awe;
Ilona,

Ilona,
Ilona,
Ilona.

1929

Funeral Eulogy

Dearly beloved, behold this man who died
and swiftly left us. We're cheated and denied.
We knew him. He wasn't great or set apart,
he was just a heart that was close to our heart.
But he's gone.
He's like the earth.
The treasure-house
has fallen in.

All of you should learn from his example then.
Such is a man. A unique specimen.
Nobody's lived like that before or since,
and as no two tree-leaves are exact prints
of each other, his like won't ever come again.
Look at this head, these dear eyes shrunk to his brain.
Behold, here is his hand, his humanness,
lost already in a fog of speechlessness,
turning into stone
like a relic bone
and on it graved in cuneiform we see
the secret sign of his one life's mystery.

Whoever he was, he was but heat and light.
Everyone knew it, spoke it: that was him all right.
As he chose this dish or other at his meal,
and as his lips spoke, that are now placed under seal
of silence, that voice which rang out merrily
—church bells drowned deep in the hollows of the sea—
and as he said, not so long ago, "Oh please,
darling, I'd like a little piece of cheese,"
and drank a sip of wine and gaily stared
at the cheap cigarette he held, that flared
and smoked, and ran to phone, and with that theme
and with those colored threads he wove his dream:

so on his forehead glowed the magic mark
that of the millions he was his one self's spark.

Look for him in vain; not here in Hungary,
not out in Asia, or in Cape Colony;
Somewhere in the past, or in the times to be
anyone could be born, but not he.
No, nevermore
will flash that strange pale smile he smiled before.
Even the ever-moving fairy luck is vain
to fix this miracle back up again.

It's all just like an old fairytale, dear friends,
and he is the man with whom it starts and ends.
Life thought him up once only, when we began
to tell these tales of him: "Once there lived a man . . . ,"
Then on him fell the cruel tonnage of the sky
and so we tell "Now he lives not . . . ," and we cry.
Here he lies, who struggled toward the better,
a statue of himself, a block of matter.
Not tears, words, nor drugs will make him rise again.
Once he lived, once he did not, here among men.

1933

Dawn Drunkenness

I will tell you. If you won't be bored by it.
Last night—at three—my work just wasn't coming
and I quit.
I lay down. But the brain's machine kept humming,
throbbed as if it couldn't stop its drumming;
I tossed and turned, bitter, exasperated;
no dream awaited.
and though I summoned it with foolish words, with counting,
with caustic sedatives, it fled my hunting.
What glared at me in fever, I had written.
With forty cigarettes my heart was smitten.
With these, and other things. Coffee. Everything.
So I get up, quite reckless now, start pacing,
clad in my nightshirt, up and down, unresting.
Their mouths slack with the honey-glazing
of sleep, my family, nested, lies embracing,
and so I stagger here, drunk brain still racing,
stare through the window-casing.

Wait. How should I start, how can I make it clear?
You know what it's like here:
you've seen the house; if only
you recall the bedroom, then you may
imagine well how at that time of day
this bleak Logodi Street lies poor and lonely.
Where you can see
into blank rooms through their windows' vacancy.

People lie blind and tumbled around me;
struck flat by sleep, their closed eyes
roll round beneath the eyelids into each head,
into the dream-world's fog and glittery lies
because the daily brain-anemia has bled

them of consciousness.
Tidied away, their shoes, clothes, all they possess,
and they themselves, lie locked up in the room,
a box which, when they waken, they'll trim and groom,
a dreamlike task in itself, but—truth to tell—
every room's a cage, each chamber is a cell.
The clock ticks out of silence, turned by its springs,
limpingly hesitates, and suddenly rings;
the roaring alarm that says
to the drowsy sleeper: "Wake up to what is."
The house too sleeps now, corpselike, senselessly,
as, in a century,
collapsed and overgrown with weeds it shall;
when nobody knows to tell
our own home from the stall of an animal.

But up there, my friend, up there is the lightening sky,
a clarity, a glittering majesty,
trembling, crystallizing into constancy.
A heavenly dome
the blue of my mother's eiderdown back home
so long ago; the water blot of monochrome
that smudged my paper-pad with an azure foam,
and the stars' souls
breathe and glitter quietly in their shoals
into a Fall night's
lukewarm mildness—which precedes the colds and whites—;
they watched the files of Hannibal, today
look down at one who, having fallen from the rest,
am standing at a window in Budapest.

And then I don't quite know what happened to me,
but a great wing seemed to swoop over me; the past,
all I had buried, bent down to me its breast:
childhood, infancy.

There so long stood I
to watch the vaulted miracles of the sky
that in the east it reddened, and the wind
set all the stars to quivering; sparks thinned
by the distance, they'd appear and disappear;
a vast thoroughfare
of light flared up, a heavenly castle door
opened in that fire;
something fluttered then,
and a crowd of guests took places to begin
deep in twilight shades of dawn
the measures of the last pavane.
Outside the foyer swam in streams of light, and there
the lord of the dance bade farewell on the stair,
a great nobleman, the titan of the sky,
the glory of the dancing-floor; by and by
there is a movement, startled, jingling,
a soft womanly whispering
miraculous; the ball is over; pages
ready at the entrance call for carriages.

Under a lace veil
streamed a mantle, fairy-tale,
from the frail
deeps of twilight, diamond-pale,
blued with such a blue
as the morning dew,
which a lovely lady dons for her surtout,
and a gem, whose hue
dusts with its light the pure peace of the air,
the otherworldly raiment she would wear;
or an angel pins, with virgin grace,
a brilliant diadem into her hair,
and a fine light chaise

rocks to a soft halt and she glides in,
quieter than a dream,
and, its wheels agleam,
on it rolls again,
a flirting smile glimpsed on the face of the queen,
and then the stallions of the Milky Way,
with glittering horseshoes gallop through the spray
of carnival confetti, each flake a star
of bright gold, where hundreds of glass coaches are.

Standing in a trance,
with joy I cried and cried out, there's a dance
in heaven, every night there is a dance;
for now a great old secret dawned on me,
that all the heavenly hosts of faerie
go home each morning on the glittery
and spacious boulevards of infinity.

I waited there
till dawn, and all I did was stare.
At last I spoke: and what then did you do
here on this earth, what worn-out stories told,
what harlotries have here imprisoned you,
what manuscript thus treasured or thus sold,
after so many summers past and winters cold,
nights idly frittered through,
that only now the dance is revealed to you?

Fifty years,
Ah, fifty years—my heart chokes in its tears—
among them, gathering, my own dead dears—
and all those fifty years, blazed on above
the host of faerie neighbors bright with love,
who see me as I rub away my tears,

and I confess that crushed and in a daze
I bowed down to the earth with thanks and praise.

Yes, look, I know there's nothing to believe,
and that this life is something I must leave,
but as my bursting heart stretched to a string,
Into that blue I could not help but sing,
that azure Him, who dwells beyond all mind,
Him, whom in neither life nor death I find.
So, though today my body is distressed,
I feel that in the dust and mire, my friend,
stumbling among lost souls, in a fruitless quest,
of some unknown and puissant Lord, yet kind,
I was the guest.

1933

ÁRPÁD TÓTH (1886–1928)

Evening Song

Behold the moon, perched on the gable's height,
Like some bizarre old tomcat, that might curl
Its golden body in a glittering ball,
Ancient and sensual sky-beast, guard of night—,
It's tired, poor thing, it's yearning for its ease:
You feel it? now it stares, determined, blind,
Would leap the window, crawl to you, and find
And rub itself around your sweet mild knees.

And look about this half-in-shadow room—
Feel how the sad old furniture tonight
Trembles toward you, stumbling would take flight
And cluster round you in a soft dark swarm:
Lonely old slaves, numb bodies crumbling,
They'd all beg refuge with you, motherless,
Ask your dear fingers for a soft caress,
To feel your gentle body's murmuring.

And see how in the darkness burn my eyes!
I lay them on your breast, jewels old and true,
Millions of years old—it comes back to you?—
They burned and hurt—were yet no earths nor skies—
They need your palm, your fingers' cool caress:
O gesture that dissolves away my being
From all else in the world that claims a being,
And rocks me in eternal blessedness.

1915

Evening Gloriole

The path ahead of us was downed with dew,
Volumes of shadow falling through the pleasance,
But still a silent gloriole wove through
The dark leaves of your hair the sunset's presence:
A mild and pensive luminosity,
Mere earthly double of the sun's rayed fullness,
Strained, by night's transmigration, variously
Into a fragrance and a perfect silence.

Fragrance and silence. Secrets, perfumy,
Gleamed in your hair, the quiet peace of heaven;
Never so sweet as then was life to me,
My heart's eyes drank the light that they were given:
And I no longer knew—if you were you,
Or if a burning bush were your dear body,
Some blessed deity's earthly form, one who
Met me in trembling leaves, half grave, half giddy?

I stood enchanted, long and silently,
The minutes as millennia extended;
You took my hand then, softly, silently,
My dazed eyelashes crept apart, unblinded;
And now I felt into my heart had come
With some deep music's fall and rise revealing,
As blood wakes veins whose paths are closed and numb,
How much I love you!—the old earthly feeling.

1924–1925

FRIGYES KARINTHY (1887–1938)

Foreword

Since I can't tell anybody
I will just tell everybody.

I tried to whisper it, lips to your ear,
To each of you, so only you could hear.

The same old secret, when all's said and done,
That no one knows, unless it's one by one.

The secret why, with darkness and with stealth,
I came into this world in blood and filth.

The word, the secret, tiny miracle,
That I might find that other, special one
And whisper in her ear: "Pass it on."

Since I can't tell anybody
I will just tell everybody.

It's surely all been blurted out anyway,
I know, but then it always stopped halfway.

One of them blushed when she heard all of this,
She'd whisper too, but it became a kiss.

The second froze to ice, as cold and numb,
Went to her grave, where I could never come.

Since I can't tell anybody
I will just tell everybody.

The third, incredulous, just looked at me,
Started to laugh; I laughed in sympathy.

When I was just a small child, I insisted
That I would speak to God if he existed.

But neither in blazing bush-light did he deign
To show himself, nor bread, nor wine,

In vain I waited in my envious greed;
He didn't honor me with faith or creed.

Since I can't tell anybody
I will just tell everybody.

It hurt me when they mocked and tortured me;
Evil would seem a better policy;

For sin's a dream, goodness a fantasy,
But more than dream is the reality

That here I am already, am still here,
Witness to how the great sun shines so clear.

No god am I, no world in all its power,
Nor north light, nor the blossoming aloe flower,

Not worse or better than another, yet
The sum of all, a living man for all that,

Neighbor and kin to every human being,
Descendant, ancestor, of all the dying,

Since I can't tell anybody
I will just tell everybody.

I'd really tell it, really utter,
But my hand limps, my mouth can only stutter.

I'd show the path to that unspoken land,
So please won't you reach out a helping hand.

Oh lift me up to speak, to live, to see,
Here in the dust no words will come to me.

I threw away my rattle, have no bell,
Down in the dust my voice lies in a spell.

A great foot pins my chest, I'm crushed in pain,
Oh lift me high where I may breathe again.

I'd rent a pulpit, there are lots for hire,
Please lead me to its steps, a little higher.

I don't yet rightly know what I will say
But I suspect glad tidings anyway,

Good news, glad tidings, secrets, a rainbow,
To you whom I have always loved,
Standing, eyes open, waiting for a miracle.

Since I can't tell anybody
I will just tell everybody.

1926

Dandelion

Why at your hand
Why at your hand, your hair
Why at your hand, your hair, your eyes
Why at your hand, your hair, your eyes, your skirt
Do I snatch so? Forever you ask,
Angrily loud at times, at times headshakingly dumb—

Why not just a gentle caress,
The way it is done by normal people,
Why so grabbingly, with those glowing eyes
And why the laughter to boot—such impertinence!
So ugly, so earsplitting, so raucous!
Oh, you'll leave me at once, or slap my hand!
Dandelion, don't leave,
Better I tell you,
I'll tell you—wait, I'll whisper in your ear—
Just push aside that curl.

What at your hand
What at your hand, your hair
What at your hand, your hair, your eyes
What at your hand, your hair, your eyes, your skirt
So plucks and snatches thus—can't you remember?
What plucks and snatches so—you still don't know?—
Though with such an angry face
You try, despite your knowledge, to avert it,
Holding back your hair, your eyes, your skirt.

At your stamen
At your stamen, pistil
At your stamen, pistil, and stem
At your stamen, pistil, stem, and petal
What snatches, Dandelion?—the wind!
The wind, the wind, the impudent crazy wind

Screaming gleefully at your annoyance.

Dandelion, what now?
This is only a breeze.
This is still mere snatching and whistling.
But I haven't yet spoken to you about my family.
Hey, listen!
My father was Mr. Howling Storm—and my mother the celebrated Ms.
    Typhoon of Arkansaw.
Then there's my brother-in-law, Funnel Cloud—
Dandelion-fluff, haven't you ever tangled and swirled aswoon
On the spin-crest of the cloud-piercing whirlwind?

Maybe you'd better not slap my hand.

1927

LAJOS KASSÁK (1887–1967)

Craftsman

Scholars we are not, nor are we meditative golden-mouthed priests,
nor heroes who with war-music's tintinnabulations go into battle
and who lie now faint and still, on the silent sea-floor, on the sun-
    dazzled mountaintops,
and the thunder-smitten battlefields over and over the whole world.
Under this firmament so blue the hours yet bathe in a damnation of
    blood . . .
But we though are distant far from all this. We sit in the dark basements
    of tenements:
mute, complete, like the indissoluble *prima materia* itself.
Yesterday we still wept, and tomorrow our works may be the marvel of
    the century.
Yes! Because out of our ugly stubby fingers fresh force is forking and
    sprouting,
and tomorrow will soon drink a pledge on the new walls.
Tomorrow with iron, asbestos, enormous bulks of granite, we will fling
    new life on the ruins
and away with the official State ornamentation! the moonlight! the stagy
    Orpheums!
Gigantic skyscrapers we shall build, and for a plaything a replica of the
    Eiffel Tower.
Basalt-booted bridges. Onto plazas of steel, steel that sings songs out of
    the new myths,
and onto dead railroad-carcasses we hurl fiery screaming locomotives,
coruscating in their completed orbits, like the eye-paining actinic
    meteors of the sky.
We mix never-before-seen colors and stretch out new cables under the
    sea
and we it is that cause the prim spinsters to be big with child, that the
    earth may nurse a new race:

that new poets may burst out rejoicing, the poets who sing before us the
  new face of the times:
poets of Rome, poets of Paris, poets of Moscow, poets of Berlin, poets of
  London, poets of Budapest.

1918

On the Fields of July

Monumentality.
Blue—blue—blue.
Geometrical fields, worlds-edge topaz yellow.
Wind. Heat. Earthsmell.
The sun trickles,
Gold planes flinging back the scarlet sun.

On these fattened and capacious fields,
Arch out now your parched and withered arms, my brothers, my sisters,
and in these yellow meadowlands behold the peasant-folk
(thigh-deep in the ripe wheatfield)
as they surge onward with a vigorous sculptural swing,
(and half-nude)
their hundredfold gesture
wiping clear the endless stretch of the fields.

Long johns, half-nude bodies. All in arms, all ready to attack. Swish.
As if the whole thing were a precise complex mechanical system,
through . . . and through the perspectival blue.

But still: (pay attention)
see the reapers' beautiful solid heads
fairly blazing out with the fresh healthy brain-marrow,
their teeth are masterpieces cut from holystone
and their calves and feet, columnar, cinnamon-brown,
root themselves at their pleasure in the black soil.

Let your eyes now drink in a billion tints and colors.
But of all of them the bread's yellow seed is the most powerful,
cut down and sheaved and tossed in crossed-stacked orderly ricks
to the song of the peasants
that their granaries should fill
and into your cologned, decrepit bodies
a new outrageous life should spring.

Wave, wave on the spacious yellow fattened land
flaglike your mad new-fashioned revolutionary tam-o'-shanters,
O brothers!

1918

MILÁN FÜST (1888–1967)

Self-Portrait

Hook-brained and gaunt
Greybeard I too would wish to be, just like the Lord Himself . . .
And were you to ask an account of my children
I would turn my head in contempt . . .

For no children have I, no part in those merry festivities,—like the
    Arabian ass
Who smelling his native land, strikes suddenly off on a different path,—
So I too set out from the way of my former security.
Nor did I choose the path of pleasure,—but that of the barren desert,
Where red are the levels of the lands and no herds graze,—
Where he who is tested must show how heavy a load he must carry.
And if the Heavenly Father gives not to eat, shall I endure it?
And thirst, shall I bewail it?
And wickedness, wander astray in it?

And in all knowledge I've sought a new thing to know,
And in every glory greater glories beyond,
And where the sky glowed sought where a greater light would glow
More burning than a woman's womb, and a darkness more profound . . .

Greybeard I shall not live to be, I see it now.
So am I to go on as before I was first turned aside? . . .
Oh grief!—maybe I could call from a window,
But fearing mockery, I creep in myself and hide.
Four walls only stare at me and glow,—
The scarlet anger of the Lord,—
Then slowly, noddingly, I rise to go
Like one who long has carried death in heart and mind,
Like an aggrieved accountant, hurt old servant,
Like one who went to seek a judge he could not find.

1932

Winter

Dark and frigid the earth. And it will be chillier still, you'll see, as in
    slow measure it turns
Slanting toward Orion's foggy projection. Touch its lumps: they too are
    dusty and chill.
And imagine: everything's going to be dustier: forever greyer will be the
    world—as if the cold
Were to permeate, pierce the essence of things, and the dust here, too,
Prevail forever . . .

So just walk on! Imagine also it's all frozen already, halted, tired of its
    wandering, stifled,—
And now already above you echoes the dry stony whirlwind of
    apocalypse where
This particular lump will fly, a blind bird,
Beaten by wind, beaten by whirlwind; turned in a cone or lashed by the
    onward rush
Of a hurricane's impetus dryly it beats and knocks unending against
    you . . .

And imagine now that I walked here too; take my heart's warmth—
Take it that I was once here, that I sang, and what melodies! I, a black
    lump of the earth, rose up
From my uttermost night, pale-faced, up to the sun, under the light . . .
And I chanted my hymns to you! and I blared them out
And left upon you my sad eyes: eternity inconsolable!

A cockfight was here, and what a fight it was! Even to remember! Two
    clumps of earth resurrected
And came against one another . . .
In thousands of sallies struck at each other, fell back suddenly;
Stared at you sometimes: unfathomable!—and called out: alas, the
    unfathomable! And their eyes, bloodshot, turned
And popped out with horror . . . there was flame, feverish chattering,—
    soul, oh orphaned wanderer,

Dust-wanderer,—slowly draw yourself out of all this, that's what I want.
    Don't watch the flames. Wait
Till we all of us turn somewhere else and forgetfulness' dust-grey cape
    and the stonestorm
Buries and covers you over.

1934

LŐRINC SZABÓ (1900–1957)

They Say, How Beautiful

They say, how beautiful, and I say nothing,
they say her bronze-blaze hair is like the dawn,
they say she carries stars in her great eyes,
that such disdain would never spare a glance for
one who's as dark and ugly as am I.
She chuckles, and they, yearning, gaze upon her,
her mocking lips, her chin's delicate arch,
and they don't know she kissed me yesterday,
and when she's silent, they can't know she's thinking
how this time yesterday the dew was falling
and how it fell on her and also me,
how seeing then our lazing afterglow
even the thrushes got intoxicated
and skimming low among the leaves of May
they burst out in a frantic madrigal.

1922

I Adore You

I adore you, I adore you,
all day long I'm yearning for you,
all day for your body sighing,
lover for his lover crying,
all day long my lips are kissing
that sweet flesh that I am missing,
kiss your every living second,
every one by kissing reckoned,
kiss the earth beneath your feet,
kiss the moment we will meet;
from afar I'm seeking for you,
I adore you, I adore you.

1928

Everything for Nothing

It's terrible, that I do see,
but it's true.
If you love me, your life should be
not unlike suicide for you.
What do I care, what the modern sect
or well-intentioned laws expect;
one must be master, one the slave;
he rules within
who serves without, whose pleasures crave
only their own law and origin.

You're not mine as long as you're your own:
your love's not real.
Want me for yourself, you weigh me down:
a holy bargain's still a deal.
Here's what I want: for you, nothing,
and in exchange, for me, everything.
All else is but two egoists
in secret strife.
I ask more: all that in you exists
must be mere components of my life.

Everyone scares me, I'm sick and tired
of the whole show.
Still, maybe, I have desired
you, but all faith left long ago.
As for these vile fears, what can I say—
there's just one way to make them go away:
in total sacrifice for me
and abjectness,
denying all the world, to be
devoted to my happiness.

Take but one moment for your own,
dare think, beget

one solitary thought alone,
feel for yourself, your life, regret;
be more than just an object, just
as dead and will-less: like the rest,
from that one moment you will be
no more, nor less,
than one more stranger is to me,
indifferent and pleasureless.

The law protects our neighbor; so
that's fine with me.
You, if you'd have me love you though,
a beast, beneath the law, must be
just like a lamp I turn off, so,
don't live unless I want you to,
don't speak, don't cry; the doorless jail
don't even see;
and on myself I will prevail
that you forgive my tyranny.

1931

Dream of the One

You being you and he being he,
his interest, not yours, he serves,
truth just a set of formulae,
or some state of the nerves;
and since the outside world won't please,
and since the masses grant no victories,
and I'd no say upon the world's decrees,
it's time for me
to liberate myself from all of you,
to loose the bonds, go free.

What am I waiting for so humbly here,
to glimpse what future times will do?
time's running, and all life is dear,
all that's alive is true.
Either I'm sick, or you are, only one;
and you tell me I shouldn't watch that gun,
whether it's love or hate that makes you run,
and I'm the prey?
if I'm the understanding one,
where does that leave me, pray?

No, no! No, I won't be just a thread
in someone else's tangled skein,
giving the guards respect and sympathy,
feeling my jailer's pain!
He who could stand it long since got away,
yes, though he walks through daggers every day.
The world and I, the two of us, must stay
stuck in this cage;
as self-concerned as is the world itself, I stand
right at the center of my stage.

See, my heart, the lock is opening,
freeing our intelligence,

which paints itself so cunningly
with bars of our pretense.
What is a thousand outside, is but one within!
Who's ever seen that fish's scale or fin
that no net, mesh untorn, could yet contain
nor filter out?
Is this forbidden? Some forbid it. Sin?
Oh certainly, if it gets out.

Within us are no borders or details,
nothing's forbidden;
it's just us—mind and soul, not good, not bad,
alone, hidden.
Hide deeper in yourself! There it will be;
that wanton reckless dawning, huge and free,
the dream that flows so endlessly
as in the acid salt
of tears and blood we taste the memory
of our dark mother, who's the sea.

Into the ocean, back forever!
Only there can we be free!
From the Many, from what's outside, we'll never
get what we need, to be.
Bargain with the masses if we must;
truth like ashes turns to dust;
our homeland is a One that will not trust
itself to be shared out;
dream then, if we can, of that true Oneness:
dream it beyond doubt.

1931

Your Name

From Cricket-Song

And if I could, I would cry out, proclaim
what is forbidden, your most secret name;
I cannot whisper, even think it, lest
—alas—I should betray it, the unguessed
yet inward-echoing secret that I claim,
the sweetness of my life, your sweetest name:
your name, sweetheart, that scrap of syllable,
that has become your elfin mask, your shell,
your soaring instrument, your precious name
that blazes round my memory in flame,
that clings like spice to me throughout the day
and makes the night a fragrant nosegay
and fastens to my mouth, and softly wreathes
my lungs, so that it's you that my chest breathes,
already almost you: each breath of mine
drinks sweetness into me, a murmured sign,
your name, that lends my heart a sweeter beat,
and only you, its secret, are more sweet.

1938

GYULA ILLYÉS (1902–1983)

Blood Kin

I'd want no more than for three days to gaze
Only upon the shady valley of your eyes,
your brows, the thick sedge of your lashes, where
the wild glint of a native water plays,
the nimble minnow-dance of your intent
that glitters, teases, in its element—
I'd want no more than this, three days together:
dumbly to gaze at one first, then the other.

And three whole days I'd spend on nothing more
than to watch wordlessly that curvature:
the soft hint of your breasts beneath your dress,
the star that has drowsed off on its caress,
and, stretching on the silk a spoke of light,
readies itself to glow on my blind night—
I'd want no more than this, three days together:
dumbly to gaze at one first, then the other.

And it had been enough for three new days
only to let my eyes go sip and graze
the beautiful twinned knees' tightbuddedness
that flaunt yet, clumsy, hide their bashfulness,
a bright portal whose double wings conspire,
perhaps, or egg each other on to flower—
I'd want no more than this, three days together:
dumbly to gaze at one first, then the other.

In the mild heat, that from your body flowed,
I would have sat, where your soft flesh-light glowed,
a convalescent patient in the sun
observing how its warmth dissolves the pain
all tingling from his poor chest where it dwelt,

how happily might this flesh also melt
into the cloudscape of a brighter sky,
which in itself is its own lullaby—

As if I were your child, in your child's place,
when I embrace you: thus I would embrace.
So what love only gives in time, I'd hear—
those solace-giving words—right now and here.
As brother sister, so I clasped you tight,
tasting that ancient yearning which absolves
the sin itself, and fell, that first strange night
into the sleep where being itself dissolves.

1932

One Sentence on Tyranny

Where there is tyranny
there there is tyranny,
not just in the rifle-barrel
nor in the jail,

nor in the chamber of inquiry,
nor in the night of the bawling turnkey,
not there only
is there tyranny,

not just in the smoky
flaming accusation,
forced confession,
Morse tapped on cell wall,

not just in the judge's Guilty!
uttered coldly
is there tyranny
nor in the soldierly

snap to "attention," "ready,"
drumroll, "fire!" and they
drag the heavy
corpse to the pit,

nor in the secretly
half-open doorway,
nor in the fearfully
whispered hearsay,

lips sealed with forefinger,
—shhh!—not only
there, is there tyranny,
nor in the hard-barred

grille of the features, set already
in the rictus of agony,
the wordless writhe of its scream,
the silence growing

with the mute tears flowing
from bulging eyes,
not there only

is there tyranny,
nor just in the heel-clicking,
the thunderous saluting,
anthems, hurrahing,

where there is tyranny,
there there is tyranny,
not just in exhausted
palms limp with applause,

in the opera's horn-calls,
the stridently lying
stone of the statues resounding, the same
in the pigments, the gallery's halls,

in every picture frame,
even the brush, the same;

not only in the midnight purr
of the gliding car,
in its halt
by the door;

where there is tyranny,
it's there in its presence
everywhere you go,
as was not even God long ago;

there's tyranny
in the kindergarten
in the advice of fathers
the smile of mothers

in how the child
answers to strangers,

not just in the barbed wire,
no less in the lines of print
than in the barbed wire,
the stupefying phrase;

there it is
in the farewell kiss
as your spouse says:
what time will you get home, love?

in the "how are you?"s
too often repeated
in the street,
the handshake suddenly gone limp,

as in an instant
your lover's face freezes,
for there it is
in the trysting-place,

not just in the interrogation,
it's there in the confession,
in the sweet word-intoxication
like a fly in the wine,

for not even in dream
can you be alone,
it's there in the wedding-bed,
and before that, in the attraction,

for you can only find lovely
what already belongs to it;
that's what you were lying with
when you thought you were in love;

in the glass, in the plate,
in the mouth, in the nose,
in the cold, in the shade,
indoors and out,

if the window's open,
it's the stench of a corpse,
if you're in the house,
somewhere there's leaking gas,

in the conversation
tyranny's asking the questions,
even in your imagination
you've no independence;

above, the Milky Way has changed:
a borderland, where searchlights sweep,
a minefield; a star
a spying window,

the crowded tent of heaven
one big labor camp;
for tyranny resounds
from fever, from bells ringing,

from the priest in confession,
from the sermon,
the church, the parliament, the rack:
they're all just theater;

close and open your eyelids:
it's still looking at you;

like a disease
or a memory, you can't shake it off;

you hear the train wheels on the rail:
they rattle at you, you're in jail, in jail;
on the mountain, by the sea
you breathe it in unceasingly;

let lightning flash, it's there
in every unexpected noise it's there,
in light's sudden stare,
in the heart's shocked startle it's there;

in peace it's there,
in this handcuffed boredom,
the endless rush of rain,
the bars reaching up to the skies,

in the cell wall,
its white imprisoning snowfall;
it looks out at you
in your dog's eyes,

and because it is in every intention
it's in your tomorrows,
in your every reflection,
your every motion,

as water its bed,
you fit and create it;
so do you try to spy out from the encirclement?—
it looks at you from the mirror,

it spies you there, you run in vain,
you're the jailed one and the jailor;
in the taste of your tobacco,
in your clothes' texture,

soaked, absorbed
in your marrow,
you think, but only its thought
comes to mind,

you think, but see only
what it conjures up for you,
and it has flamed up already in a circle,
a forest fire from a match,

for when you threw it down,
you didn't step on it;
and now it's watching out for you
in the factory, the field, at home,

and you don't feel what it means to live any more,
what bread and meat can mean,
what it means to love, to desire,
to open your arms,

handcuffs the servant
both creates and wears;
eat it, it grows,
your child you beget for it,

where there is tyranny,
everyone's a link in the chain,
from you it stinks and flows,
for you yourself are tyranny;

like a mole in sunlight
we walk in blind night,
and fidget in a room
as if in the simoom;

for where there is tyranny,
all is in vain,

even your poetry,
how true to you soever,

for there it stands
beside your grave,
it tells who you were;
even your dust obeys.

1950

Refuge

In vain you comfort me and tell me:
put up with it, it's no big thing,
but I am sick; not even you, love,
dare feign to be encouraging.
This god-damned plague, I didn't catch it
yesterday or the day before,
and there's no way for me to kick it,
it groans in what my mother bore;
and there's no analgesic for it,
its pains so many and so sore—
the hapless sufferer who's got it,
the doctors know they can't restore;
no shooing-off its horror-image
even one day, it can't be glossed;
no getting past it, we must face it,
acknowledge it: that I am lost.

    For it's an ancient woe, old age is,
its symptoms creep up, then surpass—
so terrifyingly, I tremble
to venture near a looking glass;
so he must feel, whose face with cancer
yellowing, starts to lose its bloom,
so he whose forehead with a sentence
syphilis stamps its imposthume;
naked each day against the end. So
now I behold myself, he me;
in every year beyond the fiftieth,
sooner or later, agony.

    It doesn't strengthen me to cover
my eyes from that which, frankly, I
am not at all sure, now I've seen it,
I'm really all that frightened by.

I should see, if I'm not a coward,
that which I surely cannot flee,
and you, sweet comforter, might even
with women's wisdom succor me;
I should be able, when fate's hounds have
found me and come to tear and seize,
retreat, no looking back, as I would
retreat between my mother's knees;
be able—hear the sweet old poem:
te spectem suprema mihi
cum venerit hora—"my final
hour, when departure calls on me:
to raise my eyes unto your glory"
and—*te teneam moriens*
deficiente manu—"thou shouldst
clasp my weak hands in providence."

　　Because with your angelic dictate,
you, you women, understand
how to support the bloodstained hero
just as the babe, with tender hand;
and since one bed serves love and dying,
and since however we end here,
death strips us naked and depraves us,
taints and degrades us in our fear,
and since for long now in your seeing,
my secret has no alibi,
help me then with a mother's patience
to pass the shame of death, and die.

1954

ATTILA JÓZSEF (1905–1937)

Beads

Beads around your neck aglow,
Frogheads in the lake below.
Lambkin droppings,
Lambkin droppings in the snow.

Rose within the moon's halo,
Gold belt round your waist to go.
Hempen knottings
knotted round my neck just so.

Skirted legs so subtly swinging,
bell-tongue in its bell a-ringing,
river-mirror
with two swaying poplars' winging.

Skirted legs so subtly calling,
bell-tongue in its bell a-tolling,
river-mirror
with the dumb leaves falling, falling.

Summer 1928

Night in the Outskirts

From loading-yards like deep sea caves
the light now lifts its sagging net,
our kitchen's drowned beneath the waves,
sunk in a dusk still darker yet.

Silence,—a scrub-brush almost goes
languidly to its feet, to crawl;
a bit of brick wall dimly knows
that it must either stand or fall.

Tattered, oil-soaked, now the evening
sighs in the sky and quits,
at the town's edge exhausted sits;
across the square it staggers, yawning,
then lights a bit of moon for burning.

Like ruins of the dusk they rise,
factories,
but still,
of deeper darkness yet they are the mill,
foundations of silence.

And through their windows flies in sheaves
the moonlight's frieze,
its mysteries:
out of whose woof each ribbed loom weaves
till dawn, when workaday resumes,
somberly out of gloom and gleams
the sleeping mill-girls' tumbled dreams.

A vaulted graveyard looms beyond:
lime kiln, iron mill, screw mill, silent.
Family crypts whose echoes' fiction
guards a secret resurrection:
closely whispered mysteries.

A cat investigates the fence,
a watchman, superstitious, sees
a sudden flash, will-o'-the-wisp
that glows and blinks and vanishes,—
the beetle-bodied dynamos
shine cool, obscure, immense.

Train whistle.

Dew infiltrates the dusk, and sleeves
a fallen linden's greying leaves:
dust in the roadway
clogs as it cleaves.

A muttering worker, cop upon his beat.
Comrade, with leaflets, cuts across the street.
Just as a dog
sniffs and follows what's before him,
as a cat turns back and hearkens,
circling streetlights, where it darkens.

The inn's mouth spews out light that's rotten,
its windows vomit pools of ache;
inside, the choked lamp swings forgotten,
a laborer keeps a lonely wake.
The barman wheezes in his doze;
the drunk grins at the wall's illusion,
reels on the lewd stairs, overflows,
weeps. And cheers the revolution.

The clapping water sets and chills
like smeltings in the mills.
The wind moves like a dog astray,
its great tongue touches, loose and splay,
the waters; drinks and swills.

Hay-mattresses like rafts swim mute
upon the serried waves of dark—

The warehouse is a shipwrecked bark,
the foundry's an iron barge: behold
the foundryman dreams through the mold
a scarlet babe of molten gold.

All's thick with dew, all's heaviness.
The mildew traces out the maps
of all the lands of wretchedness.
The barren fields of tattered grass
yield only rags and paper scraps.
They'd crawl if but they could. They stir,
too feeble to do more.

In whose image the soiled laundry flaps,
blown by your moist and clinging air,
O Night!
as ragged sheets hung out to dry
on life's worn clothesline of the sky,
O Grief, O Night!
Night of the poor! become my coal,
smoke hotly here upon my soul,
melt from my heart its steel, make it
the standing anvil that won't split,
the hammer's twang and glit colliding,—
in victory the forged blade gliding,
O Night!

I sleep, brothers, that I might be fresh.
The night is heavy, somber, whole.
Let not the worm devour our flesh.
Let not affliction crush our soul.

1932

The Last of Seven

Mortal dweller, may your mother
bear you seven times together!
Once within a house that's burning,
once in floods, the ice floes churning,
once in bedlam, yelling, yearning,
once in a wheatfield's soft turning,
once in cloisters bell-intoning,
once stied with pigs in grunts and groaning.
What though these six cry out to heaven?
You shall be the last of seven!

If your enemy come to hurt you,
seven there be who won't desert you:
one who starts his day off ready,
one who's on his tour of duty,
one who takes no pay for teaching,
one cast onto the waves, beseeching,
one, a seed of forests splendid,
one, bellowing ancestors defended
when all his tricks could not get even—
you shall be the last of seven!

If you're seeking for a woman,
seven seek her love in common.
One who spends his heart upon her,
one who pays his debts of honor,
one who plays the musing dreamer,
one who gropes her skirt, the schemer,
one knows where the hook is hidden,
one treads her kerchief, that's forbidden,—
as flies buzz meat, their goal and heaven!
You shall be the last of seven!

If you'd make a poet's living,
seven will work the poem-giving.

One builds towns of marble vision,
one born sleeping, a magician,
one who measures heaven's gutters,
one whose name the logos utters,
one who carves his soul a tiller,
one vivisector and rat-killer.
Four scientists, two heroes even—
you shall be the last of seven!

And if it falls as it is written,
seven to the grave are smitten:
one dandled at a milk-filled bosom,
one grasping at a stony bosom,
one who scorns the empty platters,
one ally of the poor, in tatters,
one worn to shreds by work and action,
one gazer at the moon's perfection:
may you share the tomb of heaven!
You shall be the last of seven!

1932

Ode

1.

I am alone on these glittering crags.
A sinuous breeze
floats delicious, the infant summer's
suppertime simmer and ease.
I school my heart into this silence.
Not so arduous—
All that is vanished is aswarm in me,
my head is bowed, and my hand is
vacuous.

I see the mane of the mountain—
each little leaf-vein
leaps with the light of your brow.
The path is quite deserted,
I see how your skirt is floated
in the wind's sough.
Under the tender, the tenuous bough
I see you shake out your hair, how it clings,
your soft, trembling breasts; behold
—just as the Szinva-stream* glides beneath—
the round white pebbles of your teeth,
and how the welling laughter springs
tumbling over them like fairy gold.

2.

Oh how much I love you, who've given
speech to both the universes:
the heart's caves, its trick-weaving deepenings,
sly involute lonelinesses—
and starry heaven.
As water glides from its own thunderous fall
you fly from me and we are cleft and parted,
whilst I, among the mountains of my life, still call,

still kneel, and sing, and raise the echo with my cry,
slamming against the earth and sky,
that I love you, step-nurse, mother-hearted!

3.
I love you as a child his mother's breast,
as the dumb caves their own bottomlessness,
as halls the light that shows them best,
as the soul loves flame, as the body rest!
I love you as we who marked for death
love the moments of their living breath.

Every smile, every word, every move you make,
as falling bodies to my earth, I press;
as into metal acids eat and ache,
I etch you in my brains with instinct's stress,
beautiful shapeliness,
your substance fills the essence they partake.

The moments march by, clattering and relentless,
but in my ears your silence lies.
Even the stars blaze up, fall, evanesce,
but you're a stillness in my eyes.
The taste of you, hushed like a cavern-pool,
floats in my mouth, as cool;
your hand, upon a water-glass,
veined with its glowing lace,
dawns beautiful.

4.
Ah, what strange stuff is this of which I'm made,
that but your glance can sculpt me into shape?—
what kind of soul, what kind of light or shade,
what prodigy that I, who have long strayed
in my dim fog of nothingness unmade,
explore your fertile body's curving scape?

—And as the logos flowers in my brain,
immerse myself in its occult terrain! . . .

Your capillaries, like a blood-red rose,
ceaselessly stir and dance.
There that eternal current seethes and flows
and flowers as love upon your countenance,
to bless with fruit your womb's dark excellence.
A myriad rootlets broider round
and round your stomach's tender ground,
whose subtle threadings, woven and unwound,
unknit the very knot whereby they're bound,
that thus thy lymphy cellbrood might abound,
and the great, leaved boughs of thy lungs resound
their whispered glory round!

The *eterna materia* goes marching on
happily through your gut's dark cavern-cells,
and to the dead waste rich life is given
within the ardent kidneys' boiling wells!

Billowing, your hills arise, arise,
constellations tremble in your skies,
lakes, factories work on by day and night,
a million creatures bustle with delight,
millipede,
seaweed,
a heartless mercy, gentle cruelty,
your hot sun shines, your darkling north light broods,
in you there stir the unscanned moods
of a blind incalculable eternity.

5.
So falls in clotted spatters
at your feet this blood,
this parched utterance.

Being stutters;
law is the only spotless eloquence.
My toiling organs, wherein I am renewed
over and over daily, are subdued
to their final silence.

But yet each part cries out—
O you who from the billioned multitude,
O you unique, you chosen, wooed
and singled out, you cradle, bed,
and grave, soft quickener of the dead,
receive me into you.

(How high is this dawn-shadowy sky!
Armies are glittering in its ore.
Radiance anguishing to the eye.
Now I am lost, I can no more.
Up in the world I hear it batter,
my heart's old roar.)

6.

                              (Envoi)
(Now the train's going down the track,
maybe today it'll carry me back,
maybe my hot face will cool down today,
maybe you'll talk to me, maybe you'll say:

Warm water's running, there's a bath by and by!
Here is a towel, now get yourself dry!
The meat's on the oven, and you will be fed!
There where I lie, there is your bed.)

June 1933

    *Szinva is the name of a brook in the Mátra Mountains.

Mama

On Mama now my thoughts have dawdled
all of a week. Clothes basket cradled
creaked on her hip; she'd climb the stairway
up to the drying-attic's airway.

Then, for I was an honest fellow,
how I would shriek and stamp and bellow!
That swollen laundry needs no mother.
Take me, and leave it to another.

But still she drudged so quietly,
nor scolded me nor looked upon me,
and the hung clothes would glow and billow
high up above, with swoop and wallow.

It's too late now to still my bother;
what a giant was my mother—
over the sky her grey hair flutters,
her bluing tints the heaven's waters.

October 1934

Shma Yisroel

In paupers' filthy sheets I crept
from land to land, restlessly roving,
my full heart, childlike, wailed and wept,
alone among the glad, sat grieving.
What resting place will yet accept
this weary soul?—I cried out, heaving:
Shma Yisroel!

Servants obeyed me; wife, truth-souled,
sat with me on a silken cushion
to count my oxen and my gold;
I grew in strength and erudition
and, giving alms, in joy I told
my inner soul in exultation:
Shma Yisroel!

And now, whatever there may come,
Great fame, or money, or affliction;
let them cast stones at me, or doom
for me a deathbed and destruction;
yet still I'll cry out from the tomb
love's endless words of recollection:
Shma Yisroel!

1936

Late Lament

I burn with ninety-six degrees of fever;
    Mother, you aren't nursing me.
Beckoned, you went, lay down with my bereaver,
you loose, light girl, preferred death's company.
From lovely women, autumns soft and heady,
I strive to piece you back together, yearning;
but I am running out of time already,
    near spent out with this burning.

I'd gone to Szabadszállás,* I remember,
    the last days of the wars;
for Budapest lay stricken that November,
and there was no bread in the city's stores.
I'd bought potatoes, millet tied in sacking,
I lay across a train's roof, belly-prone;
would not take "no" until I'd got a chicken,
    but when I came, you'd gone.

You stole yourself away from me, gave over
    your warm breasts to the worms.
You comforted and chid your son and lover,
and look how lying were your sweetest terms.
You cooled my soup, you stirred it and you blew it,
"Eat up, my angel, grow up big for me . . ."
and now your void mouth tastes an earthy suet—
    cheating and treachery.

I should have eaten you! . . . it was your dinner—
    did I ask you? Must you
cripple your back with laundry, breadwinner,
and use a wooden box to set it true?
Just spank me once again, I'd be exultant,
happy because I could then strike you back!
You are no good! spitefully nonexistent!
    You spoiled it all, you lack!

You, you're a bigger fraud than the deceiver
    who vows more than she gives!
You sneaked away from me, your dearest lover,
the pangs of labor and the faith that lives.
Gipsy! All that you gave, ingratiating,
you stole back in the end. Listen, I'll curse:
Mummy, you hear? the sound of a child, hating.—
    So scold me! Make it worse!

My mind is slowly clearing, slowly dawning,
    the sad old myth must die.
The child sees now how foolish is his yearning,
must learn to let his mother's love go by.
Man born of woman must be disappointed:
she will cheat him, or he her, at the last.
In struggle, or in peace, he is appointed
    to taste the selfsame dust.

1935; December 1936

*A small town in Hungary.

Welcome for Thomas Mann

Just as a tired child when put to bed
and tucked in snug, a stubborn sleepyhead,
still begs, "Don't go away, tell me a story"
(lest night should fall on him in sudden fury),
and while his little heart, congested, pants,
and even he knows not just which he wants,
the story, or your stay; may we prevail
on you to sit with us and tell a tale.
Tell us the old story, we won't forget,
how you've been with us always, will be yet,
how we are with you, an unparted whole,
whose cares are worthy of a human soul.
You know it well, the poet never lies;
tell the full truth, not only that which is,
tell of that light which flames up in our brain:
when we're apart in darkness we remain.
As Hans Castorp through Madame Chauchat's flesh,
let us tonight see through ourselves afresh,
your words, like pillows, muffle out the din—
tell us the joy of beauty, and the pain,
lifting our hearts from mourning to desire.
We've laid poor Kosztolányi in the mire,
and on mankind, as cancer did on him,
horrible monster-states gnaw limb by limb,
and we, aghast, ask what's the next disease,
whence fall new wolvish ideologies,
what newer poison boils within our blood—
how long, and where, you can still read aloud? . . .
So. When you speak, we must not lose our flame,
we men should still be men in more than name,
and women still be women—lovely, free—
because true humans daily cease to be . . .
Sit down. Start our favorite story—please.

We'll listen; happy he who only sees
your face among our race of evil will,
to know there's one true European still.

Early January, 1937

For My Birthday

Upon my thirty-second year—
what a surprise, this poem here,
    knicky-
    knacky:

a little gift with which I say,
lurking alone in this café:
    happy
    happy.

Thirty-two years just blew away,
I never made ten doits a day:
    hungry,
    Hungary.

A pedagogue I might have been,
not this pen-busting, might-have-been,
    saddie
    laddie.

But no; Herr College Chancellor
showed me the outside of the door:
    mocktor
    Doktor.

It was a short sharp shock for sure,
my father-poem got its cure;
    his word
    and sword,

that saved the fatherland from me,
evoked my spirit and set free
    its name
    and flame.

"As long as I have any say
you'll not teach here a single day"—

    bibble-
    babble.

If Mr. Antal Horger's pleased
our poet's grammar-study's ceased—
    folly's
    jollies—

no high school, but a nation I,
although he like not, by and by
    shall teach,
    shall teach.

April 11, 1937

(Who Would This Poem . . .)

Who would this poem's reader be,
must know its poet, must love me,
sailing upon the vacuum,
knowing, as seers do, what's to come;

for he has dreamed, thus fathomless,
in human form a quietness,
and in his heart will come and go
the tiger and the gentle doe.

Early June, 1937

(No Flowers, but a Spike . . .)

No flowers, but a spike, you proffered,
scorn to the other world you offered,
gold you promised her who suffered,
her, your mother; now you squat,

mad toadstool in the roots, and glower
(appear thus to your anxious knower),
locked up inside the Seven Tower,
where hope is void, escape is not.

With milk teeth, why did you bite granite?
Your daydream errand, why begin it?
Why, too late, try to save a minute?
What did you want then, after all?

Your nakedness you always flaunted,
tore off the scabs from wounds you vaunted,
you're famous, if that's what you wanted.
And have you done your time? You fool.

Did you give love? Who would embrace you?
Fugitive! who would even chase you?
Just make the best of what will face you:
no breadknife, and of course no bread.

You're in the Seven Tower for good.
Be glad if you have firewood,
glad for a pillow to your bed,
be a good boy, lay down your head.

November 24, 1937

(And So I've Found My Native Country . . .)

And so I've found my native country,
that soil the gravedigger will frame,
where they who write the words above me
do not for once misspell my name.

This black collection box receives me
(for no one needs me any more),
this Iron Six that was worth twenty,
this coin left over from the war.

None needs that iron ring inscripted
with sweet words, that the world is new:
rights, land.—Our laws are the leftovers;
now pretty gold rings all pursue.

For many years I had been lonely.
Then many people visited.
I'd have been happy if they'd stayed.
You are alone, was what they said.

And so I lived, useless and empty,
and now I see it all quite plain.
They let me play the fool until
by now even my death's in vain.

All through my life I've tried to weather
the whirlwind that would always blow.
I was more sinned against than sinning,
and it's a laugh that it was so.

Spring, summer, autumn, all are lovely;
but winter's loveliest for one
who hopes for hearth and home and family
only for others, when all's done.

November 24, 1937

MIKLÓS RADNÓTI (1909–1944)

Psalms of Devotion

1.

Through ravaged and love-torn lips our words,
even, our spinning, our surcharged words,
englobe themselves into kisses, they
hide and go seek in our marveling
one-in-the-other-betangling
eyes, behind elegant ormolu
eyelashes fade away soundlessly;
for they're born to an exquisite gift,
psalmed visions, a sophistical kiss,
on whose thick trunk the yellow thrushes
in chattery fluttering couple.

August 27, 1929

2.

Long-ago stars that were snatched
sparkling from skyfields now struggle,
prying my fingers, to
flee; so much I love you
    you see
big with its lifefruit, my joy,
harvest-ripe, bunches, and eared,
bends with the weight of the grain;
silent at night I imprint,
press with my kisses my tongue's
dusky adoring, its red
utterance into your palm.

December 10, 1928

3.

Sometimes your warm little hands are
cold at the fingerpeaks, musical spires,

tips of my slender existence—as
rich in vaporous colors as
opulent kisses bestowed in silence—
lacily trimmed with your breathtaking sighs,
ardently taken, my big, white,
moist teeth chattering away in my head.

May 26, 1929

4.
Goldening orange glows in your slender
fingers the ancient delight of our lives,
why, because long, long ago we marveled to-
gether deep in the drenched and amazing
groves at the birds, at their hot
colorful warbling nest-making.

Hot in the pit of your palm the forests
tell of abundant original
sky-worlds we plummeted down out of,
two white and innocent virgins,
flowers without peer, that faded the moment they
blew, for immaculate thus was con-
ceived our miraculous beautiful
child in the lap of the leaf-falling groves.

February 7, 1929

5.
As bellowed sky-blue by a new-born god,
gorgeous-voiced organs roar within my body,
all my dream-mountains cave in one by one,—
lately you came to me, a fallen star
as stars in Fall, because I love you so
I carry in my eyes that life eternal
belonging to the snowy-bearded gods
and thus I learn your kisses' sacrament,

your priest!
as wise old women tell our fates in cards.

June 25, 1929

6.
Pale demi-moons, only our fingernails glimmer;
eyes' cumbrous curtains are lowered, and we
play at our loving with hands that are blind;
for only thus will the violet birds
appear in the fog of the lamplight; if our
eyes, speechless, opened, they'd be walled by a mist:
now, demi-moons, only our fingernails glimmer.

March 5, 1929

7.
Sometimes we bite. On our teeth's glittering
armor chattering shatters a kiss:
a tiny garland of blood-drops flutters
over the arch of the eyebrow.
A star is crawling and crawling
the sky and under our lovemaking
reverent curtsies the grass; and clinging,
clinging, the thickets blow in the wind,
as sometimes the tongues of innocent lovers
cling when they touch in their kissing.

July 9, 1929

8.
You! You're an earth-sweet meadow, your panting's as simple as
that of a lovemaking farmboy; your body carries
sacred the curse, the ancient power of the earth-mother.
Sometimes the bell of your fleshly will clangs
alone, and I'm called to Mass in the silence
breathing beneath the gasping tower of dark.

Your love descends on me circling, as the great
leaf of a wild chestnut falls. As now.
In sadness's clean and translucent dawning
you're the earth, the body, the blood,
and compared to you all is nought but a game.

July 12, 1928

Canticle

You are trunk and root,
plenteous leaves and fruit,
and the cooling breeze,
the warm sun, ripening,

root that binds and heals,
blood that runs and trills,
slim and branchy bole,
O you wind-befriending,

leafdress of my limbs,
run into my arms,
blossom of my breast,
heart's coverlet and cling,

you're the waking sun
in the shining dawn,
fruit of all my leaves,
with me awakening,

as with me in deep
heart-enfolding sleep,
sweet peace of evening,
silent pulse repeating,

wordloveliness's spring,
shriek-engendering,
winged and feathered breath,
with spirit's fluttering,

light within the shade,
brighter than a blade,
dark jewel in the light,
O smoky cloudying,

evelight as it glows
on your eyelid's close,
rock me in your arms,
your body opening,
O blessing in life's war,
smile hidden at the core,
who shall among my bones,
anciently whitening
on the cold earth's stones,
hide you forevermore.

March 8, 1935

Just Walk On, Condemned to Die

Just walk on, condemned to die!
In woods where winds and cat screams wail,
sentence in darkened lines
shall fall upon the pines;
hunchbacked with fear the road turns pale.

Just shrivel up, you autumn leaves!
Shrivel, most hideous of worlds!
Cold hisses from the sky;
on grasses rusted dry
the shadow of the wild geese falls.

O poet, live as clean as those
hill-dwellers in their windblown snows,
O live as free of sin
as baby Jesus in
an ikon where the candle glows,

as hard as the great wolf who goes
wounded and bleeding through the snows.

1936

Twenty-nine Years

*For Gyula Ortutay**

Twenty-nine! a week now since my birthday;
always I have celebrated,
marked with poems those monstrous turning-places,**
one for every year accumulated;
but now that comfort, which has never
failed before, is quite belated,
seems to have abandoned me forever.

So throughout the last night of my twenties
I mumbled counting till the morning,
heaped the nines upon the wretched twenties
—all I got was thirty. Years keep turning;
years I've lived like this, distress
every year my heart tormenting,
pure as Crusoe in his wilderness,
getting by, but gradually learning
this: that nothing will protect him
when the hunters come to fell this treehouse,
loose the clamorous dogs against him;
hunters steeped in beastliness,
blood shed by the bleeding sunset,
eavesdrop in his simple blamelessness.

Sleeplessly I lay there in the turning
and the sway of vertigo,
on my eyelids weary lights were falling,
then a sudden rain, and in its flow
the night welled up, its chilly welter
washed a star onto my window,
drove the torpid moths indoors for shelter;
one moth drifted down, so evanescent,
one deathless star looked in at me;
how many years have I been present?

Twenty-nine? A snow-white entropy
lifts me up, caresses me,
a frail flake in the wind's soft pressure,
rocked in its dreadful leisure languidly.

So I rose. A vague and spectral dawning
walked the hunchbacked hill's illusion;
standing at my window in the morning,
had I twenty years left? ten? or maybe none?
Does it matter what the number?
—not as if you had collected
cold possessions in this little chamber,
fine possessions—nothing evil ever
took its root in your desire;
still they hunt you, whether knife or cancer,
does it matter? Say perhaps the fire
needs your poems in the end,
say you never touched the lyre,
the unborn poems would whistle in the wind.

See, the moth is dying, but the starry
light lingers through time and tide;
a mighty river pours unceasingly,
its marshy delta sighs, the ripples glide,
the waters dream, and from the flow
of brilliant swaying reeds floats up
toward the sun a roseate flamingo.

May 1938

*Gyula Ortutay was one of Radnóti's best friends.
**Radnóti's mother and identical twin brother died in childbirth.

Foamy Sky

The moon sways in a foamy sky.
How strange that I'm alive. A bland,
efficient death searches this age,
and they turn white on whom it lays its hand.

Sometimes the year looks round and shrieks,
looks round and faints away.
What kind of autumn lies in wait,
what winter dulled with agony to grey?

The forest bled, and every hour
in that revolving time bled too.
The wind was scrawling numbers, huge
and darkening in the unsettled snow.

I have seen certain things, such things
that now the air feels dense as earth.
A rustling tepid silence holds
me fast, as in that time before my birth.

I come to a standstill by this trunk.
It stirs its thick leaves angrily,
reaches a branch down—for my neck?
Now I am neither weak nor cowardly,

just tired. Unmoving. And the branch
searches my hair, terrified, mute;
such things one must forget, but I
have never yet been able to forget.

Foam gushes forth upon the moon.
A dark green venom streaks the sky.
I roll myself a cigarette,
am slowly, carefully, a living I.

June 8, 1940

Calendar

January
Sunrise is late, and the dark,
the denseness, comes up to the brim of heaven.
It's so filled up with the black
that it's ready to spill.
The step of the dawn on the ice
crackles its colorless chill.

February 5, 1941

February
Having glided, and swayed, and settled, the snow
is melting already, the flow
carves out a passage;
sunbeams are gleaming, skylights are beaming,
the sunbeams wink in their gleaming.
Listen, the white-voiced sheep
bleat their woolly reply;
chirping, the sparrow ruffles its wings at the sky.

February 21, 1941

March
Look, the puddle's got goose pimples!
March and its boisterous
breezes play under the trees, simply
yelling like roisterers,
The chilly bud has not unbuttoned,
nor spider spun its caul,
but chicks run everywhere, each one
a golden yellow ball.

February 26, 1941

April
A barefoot breeze winces on broken glass. A squeal;
limping, it runs away.
O April, April, what is this?
The sun won't shine, the buds delay—
no hint of leaves or flowers their dripping snouts reveal
under the whistling sky.

March 12, 1939

May
The petal shakes, falls from the bough;
in blanching fragrances the dusk comes now.
Deep in the chilly mountain breeze
wade richly laden avenues of trees.
The warm air shivers, steals away;
the chestnut-candles glimmer, lift and sway.

February 25, 1941

June
Behold the noon in its miraculous power:
above, the flawless and unwrinkled sky;
along the roads, acacias in flower;
the stream throws out a comb of golden ply,
and in the brilliance, bold calligraphy
is idly, glitteringly, written by
a boastful, diamond-budded dragonfly.

February 28, 1941

July
Scowling, colicky, the cloudpack
claps the air.
Showers, barefoot, dance around,

naked white, with soaking hair.
Tired with this, they go to ground;
evening light.
Summer, clean-limbed, leans between the
sycamores, their faces bright.

June 12, 1940

August
Upon the matted meadows
the blaring sunshine beams;
and yellowing in leafshade
the golden apple gleams.
The squirrel squawks; within the glowing
chestnut, prickly globes are growing.

July 21, 1940

September
O how can I have lived all these Septembers!
Under the trees brown gems, the starry embers
of chestnut-falls—evoking Africa,
her fiery veins! Before the cooling rains.
Dusk makes its bed among the fading clouds,
on the exhausted trees falls a veiled glow;
with hair undone the sweet Fall enters now.

July 15, 1940

October
Cold and gold the blustering,
wanderers rest from wandering.
Mouse in pantry gnaws its cheese,
gold is burning in the trees.
All is golden-yellow, where
yellow corn does not yet dare

pawn the fawnsilk gonfalon:
so it flaunts its raingold awn.

February 7, 1941

November
The frost has come, it shrieks upon the wall;
Listen! the teeth of skulls are chattering.
Among the branches, sere and brown with Fall,
grey wisps of crazy mirth are pattering.
And do I fear the owl's foreboding call?
Perhaps. Perhaps not at all.

January 14, 1939

December
No more than a wraith at noon,
the sun is a silver full moon.
Mist, like a torpid bird, glides.
Snow falls through the night;
an angel soughs in the gloom.
Silent through drifting snow
death in its nakedness strides.

February 11, 1941

Winter Sun

The melting snow collapses,
slinks softly to and fro,
the kettles steam like pumpkins
baked scarlet, sliced to go.

The icicle, extending,
Lets its drop magnify,
And now a puddle splashes
And gazes at the sky.

Up on the shelf of heaven
the snow slides further on;
scarce-worded I'm becoming,
all argument is gone.

I line up for the noon-meal,
or do I wait to die?
Between the night
-and-day world
my chafing soul must fly.

My shadow glances at me,
the winter light's undone,
my cap is regulation,
a hat upon the sun.

1942

Paris

Where the Boul' Mich' meets the Rue
Cujas the corner slopes perceptibly.
Lovely wild youth, I have not left you,
your voice, like echoes in a gallery,
a shaft, beats through the caverns of the heart.
At Rue Monsieur le Prince the baker plied his art.

In the park, leftwards, one of the tall
trees has shimmered yellow to the sky
as if it felt the chill of Fall.
Liberty, long-thighed nymph, O lovely shy
one clad in your dusk-goldening chemise,
are you still hiding in the veiled, the shrouded trees?

The drums of summer marched and beat,
sweated, and raised the dust upon the road.
Cool vapors followed; soft and sweet
from both sides now a subtle fragrance flowed.
Noon was full summer; cool in the evening
with rainy brow the autumn came a-visiting.

I took my pleasures where I found
them, like a child, or like an erudite
old sage who knows quite well the world is round.
How green I was! my beard was snowy white.
I wandered where I would and no one frowned.
Then I descended to the torrid underground.

Where are you now, echoing metro stations:
CHÂTELET-CITÉ-ST. MICHEL-ODÉON!
DENFERT-ROCHEREAU sounding like imprecations?
Maps flowered on the dirty walls. How long,
how long! I cry out. Hush, I'm listening:
that smell of sweat and ozone starts its whispering.

And O the nights! The nightly wandering
from the far outskirts to the Quartier!
And shall the strangely clouded dawn yet bring
to Paris once again those pales of grey
when I'd undress for bed so sleepily,
dazed and still drunk with writing poetry?

Had I but strength, O would I might go back
against the heavy current of my fate!
The vile café downstairs employed a black
cat that climbed the rooves to copulate.
And shall I hear again that yowl and croon?
That was the very moment that I learned how great
a din there was when Noah swam beneath the moon.

August 14, 1943

The Fifth Eclogue *(fragment)*
In memory of György Bálint*

Cold, how shuddering cold, my friend, was the breath of this poem,
with what dread did I fear its words; and today again I have fled them,
scribbling half-lines.
          And always of some other thing, *of some other thing,*
I would write, but in vain! The night, this night with its hidden prodigies
summons me: write about him.
              And I startle, and rise, but the voice
already has ceased, like the dead among the Ukrainian corn.
Missing.
          Nor has the autumn brought news of you.
                      Now in the forest
again rustles the shelterless omen of winter; the clouds draw on,
heavy with snow, and slowly come to a halt in the sky.
And are you alive?
           Not even I can know that, nor can I
rage when they throw up their hands and bury their face in despair.
They can know nothing.
              But are you alive? Only wounded, perhaps,
are you wading the leaf-drift, the fragrant mold of the forest? Or are you
no more but the fragrance?
             Already the fields flutter with snow.
Missing,—the word
          Stiffens and chills in the thud of the heart
and there in the ribs' cage the twisted anguish awakens,
and now my memory shivers, delivers your words from the past
in a pain so sharp I can feel the touch of your physical being
as that of the dead—
          yet I can't write about you, I just can't.

November 21, 1943

   *György Bálint was Radnóti's friend. He died as a Jewish labor serviceman in the Ukraine.

À la Recherche . . . *

Gentle old evenings, you ennoble yourselves into memory
with the glittering table, with poets and young wives garlanded,
but whither are all of you gliding, mired in the past?
Whither that night when the quickened companions would pledge
their friend the Grey Friar** from the slender golden-eyed glasses?

Verses swam in the lamplight; glimmering green
adjectives danced on the froth and comb of the meter, and
the dead were alive, the prisoners home, the missing
belovedest friends so long ago fallen were writing;
on their hearts lies the soil of Hispania, Flanders, Ukraine.

Some of them gritting their teeth would plunge in the fire
and went into war compelled, they could do no other;
while the squad around them slept uneasily, under
the cover of dirty nights they remembered their rooms
that had been for them island and cave in this age of the world;

some, in a certain place, traveled in sealed boxcars,
unarmed they stood paralyzed, silent, out in the minefields;
and some, in another, went willingly, armed, as silent,
knowing this struggle here below was their own,
and nightly the angel of freedom guards their great dream.

And some, . . . but what matter. Whither the wise wine-drinking?
The draft cards were flying, fragments of poems multiplied;
so also the creases around the beautiful smiles
and under the eyes of the girls; heavy their fairy-
light footsteps became in the silent years of the war.

Where is that night, that inn, that table under the lindens,
and where are the living, where the trampled in battle?
My heart hears their voices, my hand preserves their hands' pressure,
I summon their lines; their proportions loosen, I seek
their measure (dumb prisoner), here on the sad heights of Serbia.

Where is that night? That night will never return,
for what happened takes on from death another perspective:
there they are, sitting at table, hidden in girl-smiles,
and they'll drink yet from this glass who sleep unburied
in forests deep and remote, and in foreign fields.

Lager Heidenau: in the mountains above Zagubica. August 17, 1944

*This is one of the ten poems inscribed in Radnóti's address book that was found in
the pocket of his raincoat, when his mass grave was exhumed in 1946.
** Name of a Hungarian white wine.

Razglednicas*

1.

Rolling from Bulgaria the brutal cannonade
slams at the ranges, to hesitate and fade;
men and beasts and carts and thoughts are jammed into one,
neighing the road rears up, the maned sky will run.
And you're the only constant in the changing and the mess:
you shine on eternal beneath my consciousness;
mute as an angel wondering at the catastrophe,
or the beetle of burial from his hole in a dead tree.

*In the mountains.** August 30, 1944*

2.

At nine kilometers: the pall of burning
hayrick, homestead, farm.
At the field's edge: the peasants, silent, smoking
pipes against the fear of harm.
Here: a lake ruffled only by the step
of a tiny shepherdess,
where a white cloud is what the ruffled sheep
drink in their lowliness.

*Cservenka.*** October 6, 1944*

3.

The oxen drool saliva mixed with blood.
Each one of us is urinating blood.
The squad stands about in knots, stinking, mad.
Death, hideous, is blowing overhead.

Mohács. October 24, 1944

4.†

I fell beside him and his corpse turned over,
tight already as a snapping string.
Shot in the neck. "And that's how you'll end too,"

I whispered to myself; "Lie still; no moving.
Now patience flowers in death." Then I could hear
"Der springt noch auf,"†† above, and very near.
Blood mixed with mud was drying on my ear.

Szentkirályszabadja. October 31, 1944

Razglednica means "picture postcard" in Serbo-Croatian. These are the last four poems Radnóti inscribed in his address book on the death march.
**Radnóti's camp was located in the mountains.
***The German guards killed 1,000 to 1,200 Jewish servicemen at Cservenka.
†This is the last of the poems Radnóti composed on the death march.
††In German, "He is still moving."

ISTVÁN VAS (1910–1991)

Ode to the Mind

The ancient greed of matter, spawning, slaughtering,
—Silent, ancestral—and the tyrant-hearted zeal
Enkindled by the putrid scum accumulating
Within the earth's entrails since time's beginning
Behold the flogging forces of this world that rule
The puerile fluffy folly of engendering,
Pretend to leap, dance, caper in a prancing reel.

Among them, though, is heard a new uneasy voice
That feigns as if its pupil spirit were of old,
The youngest force that ever blazed into the world,
That hides behind a glass its lovely gleaming eyes,
And steps with care in the false beard of its disguise,
Wears a grey suit—the beasts would tear it uncontrolled
Did they its secret fragile weakness realize.

O mind, young mind, a mere half-million years of age:
That you might come to be, the mammals grew the brain!
Reasons now, arguments, bite at our cells' dumb cage:
Existence's great, stubborn, docile revolution.
You, no amoeba guessed at, nor did any stone;
Without you would have failed all birth and generation
When the long ice ages ravaged the Pliocene.

After the havoc, through a crack that nature cut,
Quietly you stepped in. The moon, the earth, the sea
Groaned in their labor pains. On two feet Man stood out
Among the dying ancient beasts. And since that day
Your voice was always audible, and patiently
Never falls silent till it finds a hearer; but
Grotesque beliefs, insulted instincts ossify.

You are the anxious teenage fever-fit of being,
The lightning bolt that slashes deep into the core;
Your scissors cut the track for nature's growth and freeing,
Releasing her most hidden, rare, and lovely flower.
Not what's eternal, not what's fugitive and fleeing,
Only what it can be, become, what's in its power:
Rambling wild mind, to me you're faith itself undying.

I praise you in the jail, in war I praise your name,
Remember you among the lies, in deep earth chill;
With a split consciousness, and fallen into shame,
Stuttering, mindless, compromised, I bless you still,
And when in void dances the liberated soul,
I'll seek you in the light beyond the night, nor claim
Nor even need a God unless through your own will.

As, after mating, pleasure's drug and opiate
Exchanges to the forms of purifying consciousness:
In the wild underworld, through the huge night's distress,
Upon that perilous path don't leave me desolate.
Above the grave-pits, under the unending stars,
You, the undreamed-of link, that mad connectedness,
The most courageous passion of our human state!

1947

The Translator's Thanks

I give you thanks, benign and gentle giants,
That silenced I could speak, nor lacked for air,
That my banned voice through yours voiced its defiance,
Schiller and Goethe, Shakespeare, Molière!
I'd not be one to echo, then, full-throated,
The floodtide choiring of the fulsome lie;
Instead, furtive, in foreign lines I quoted
Piecemeal the secrets I existed by.

When I translated Nero's despotism
Before me functioned that of my own time;
In Tacitus's solid aphorism
I was set free to tell of it in mime.
My blinded stress, that anxious elevation
That comes from pained disgust, was rendered real
In Villon's lonely falcon-scream, whose passion
Announced that I had never made a deal.

Faithful to all in the old text explicit,
The new experience could find a way:
Just what I saw—that could alone elicit
What *William Tell*'s poor peasants had to say.
Once I had loosed the anger that arises,
I went, as they had done, off the deep end:
I saw the hat that in a hundred guises
The Emperor's margrave stacked wherever I turned.

How many new things did my thought and feeling
Lock into the old masterworks' alloy?
How much did I stamp into their annealing,
Tartuffe mixed with the Party's solemn lie?
But while my rhyme, with Molière's whip a-snapping,
Upon the unsuspecting stage lashed out,
I watched lest sneaking zeal, always eavesdropping,
Had cast the holy hook into my throat.

Because I couldn't change nor see commuted
My nature's secret bent, that which in me
Is individual and persecuted
Fled along ways unguarded, dark, and free:
My trembling lawlessness, late-come and wary,
Fled to the sunshine of a long-past scene,
Where heroines and heroes might unbury
Their authors, Goethe, Shakespeare, and Racine.

Invisible the wall I looked through always
To westward, westward—was it all in vain?
But Thackeray would set me in his post-chaise
And bear me to the West, to his domain.
My wishes, sunlit, fell to the seduction
Of *Henry Esmond*'s sentences and sense,
And on the road of glory and of action,
I rode that punishable elegance.

He lies, who lives; unless they have elected
That you're an embalmed mummy, dead and safe;
But in Hungarian you are resurrected
By my will's force and galvanizing life.
I owe you thanks for this your sanctuary,
Where true to you, as true to me I stay;
Into the future's oceans now you carry
The waves my heart sends from its secret bay.

Thanks, that through you I could affect the nation
By those lost times I won back through your power,
And to these days, steaming with their contagion,
Could bring the ocean wind and the free air;
Thanks, that from prison I can still keep peering,
And can entrust my message to your hand,
You gentle giants, generous and cheering,
And to world literature, our common land.

1952

JÁNOS PILINSZKY (1921–1981)

Conquer Me

Conquer me, Night!—whose dark waves swim
About my body, loose and dim,
I stepping into your long flow.
Within you all the silent poor
Roll broodingly for evermore
Their wan hearts' burdens to and fro.

Above this ragged world you turn
Forever changing, and yet one,
A gentle comfort still remain;
When all things crumble, you abide;
What your soft power casts aside
Crumbles to ashes, all in vain.

But you live yet, announce your power
In your great constellations' fire,
Paradigms ancient, still, and true;
As the first angels, so too I
Came from, and am from that dark sky:
Seize me, invade me through and through!

Forget then my unfaithfulness;
Forces unconquered, masterless,
Still lead me back to you again;
Be you a river, I the foam,
Accept your prodigal come home,
You somber, dark empyrean.

1943

On the Third Day

At dawn among the trees of Ravensbrück
The ashen skies resound. Beneath the ground
The tree-roots feel where that first light has struck.
And the wind rises. And the worlds resound.

So wretched mercenaries choked his breath,
So maybe then his heart stopped beating—ah,
But on the third day he defeated death,
Et resurrexit tertia die.

1959

On a Forbidden Planet

Born upon a forbidden planet,
pursued, I trudge the shore's sea-wrack;
the foam of heavenly nothing's caught me,
toys with me now, and throws me back.

I don't know why must I do penance—
all here's a hissing riddle-play;
whoever tracked me to this seashore,
this sunk beach, shouldn't run away.

Nor should you fear me, do not flee me,
better to hush the pain of life;
with closed eyes you should press me to you,
press me daringly, like a knife.

I never wished that I be born here,
by nothing was I birthed and fed;
love me then darkly, sharply, cruelly,
as the bereaved one loves his dead.

1943

ÁGNES NEMES NAGY (1922–1991)

Thirst

How to say it? The word can't find my mouth:
thirst for you mutes my tongue with drouth.
—Were I a pitcher-plant you'd fall in, lie
mired in my body's fragrance, quite sucked dry.
And so I would possess your warm brown skin,
your nervous hand that guards you even in
that final toppling moment, saying then:
see, I am still myself, I still remain.
Mine then your arm, bent over my arm there,
mine the black gleaming feathers of your hair,
that swish as if a wind, swishing with me,
in swinging landscapes, shining endlessly.
And so I would drink in your melting flesh
thick like the tropics, sweet and dense and fresh,
your magic fragrance, shuddering from the mage,
the horsetail and the ancient meadow-sage.
And as your weightless soul now dwells in me,
(above you like a lantern floating free),
all this, greedy, unsated, I'd devour,
as if my flesh were a carnivorous flower.
Is there no more? then peace I must despair.
I love you. You love me. There's no repair.

1942–1946

To Freedom

Cathedral! You are full of wondrousness!
What ripply-pleated angels! Lovely glances!
Seen from here the soles of a giantess,
their heads pin-like in their far radiances.

Beyond the dome flares further scenery,
Between the columns flames a painted sky:
What if I disbelieved, but you should be,
or you were not, but a believer I?

Remains of God! Your yearning dragged me yet.
You bore me now. Mad me, I don't chase after you.
Some friends of mine just starved. I mention it
because you evidently did not know.

What last straw did they chew, upon their knees?
With what mouths, set in what unfleshly skulls?
—You might have spared for them a cup of peas,
you might have managed some small miracles.

I would have liked to see their mouths once more,
their warm chins, that were shattered in their blood—
enough; I yearn for Rome, its gardens, where
I would be fed with thick and wondrous food.

Give a banana! Meat! Be the world's teat!
At night, give Naples, Switzerland at dawn!
Give vibrant air above the flowering mead,
false lying lover, you for whom I yearn!

Give a balloon! Faith! Heavenly images!
Break your own law! Give us yourself instead!
Don't let the greedy eat the people's cheese,
Bring on the resurrection of the dead!

—A peony stands upon my tabletop,
its beauty self-substantial as a gem,
its lovely petals richly frilling up
in double volutes, crowding round the stem.

If there might be some sense of adoration,
before this on my buckling knees I'd fall:
pin but on this your glorious vindication,
for it is beauty, life, and has no soul.

1942–1946

ZSUZSA BENEY (1930–2006)

From the Cycle of Mourning

I can't bear that your dying doesn't hurt me.
You aren't with me, but you haven't gone.
I who basked in the warm glow of your dwelling
swim now in winter's frozen clouds alone.

Then was it better when I fell through tearing
briars into our unveiled future, its bite
of flaming horror, than to wander
on this soft shore where neither day nor night

are able to dissolve this crystal greyness—
mirroring how you are not, but you are?
here, under the sky's vault, unruffled nothing;
perhaps those cold flakes melt to tears up there.

To lie down by you then would have been better—
to feel, upon the shivering flesh of me,
your unmoved corpse, than this, this beating
on my mouth, this thick-sweet insanity.

Published 2008

From the Cycle "It Twinkles but Disappears"

You stop, look round, and turn to step once more
through the pearl curtain of the door of being;
now visible, now but a shade you walk
over the edge of two worlds.

You as in falling snow pass hindranceless
right through the black-white grid of checking bars.
On both worlds pelts each other's meltingness,
impenetrableness.

And I don't know if still in its dark royal
shreds the city stands yet, or if the wind
lashes the empty fields—I don't know whether
I am receding from or running to you,

for in this darkling falling time the world's
collapsing back into its elements.
To snow, to dark. There's no one to rekindle
one more winter's dawn.

1982

ÁGNES GERGELY (1933–)

You Are a Sign on My Doorpost
For my dead father

I haven't any memories,
and if I do I don't hold onto them.
I don't prowl sniffing in the cemeteries,
I'm not moved by organic chemistry.

But sometimes, when November comes,
and it gets foggy, and behind the clammy pane
I find myself gasping for lack of air,
—the place your body lies unknown—
tracking some kind of vegetative memory
one of your gestures oozes, oozes up.
I feel how in your long and nervous fingers
a thermos turns, a bad can opener,
a pocket knife, a backpack with an open mouth,
one pair of undershorts, a prayer book,
and taking on the weightless weight your back
creakingly finds it still can carry it.
I feel you're setting out, the well-dressed wayfarer:
you never take the trip, only set out on it.
You laugh, you look back, you are only thirty-eight;
I'll be back soon, you nod, and point—
next day would have been your birthday—
and whimpering inwardly, like a picture by Mednyánszky,
you wave—and how you wave!

Your sign is on my doorpost: you cling on yet;
Ferdinand Bridge, the palm-sized grating,
the slushy road, the inanition, crazed grass-eating,
all of them only lucubration,
for I lied. I keep on seeing you;
under that strangling November sky

I'm with you as you start, you're breathing and it's you,
your tears that choke my throat, I leave them as they are,
and up above, there where it flew,
that slender cigarette knocked out of your mouth
burns through the skin, on a star.

1963

Isabel and Ferdinand

1492

Isabel and Ferdinand—
To the garden hand in hand,
Valladolid's garden-ground,
Went Isabel and Ferdinand.

From this union issued Spain:
What was two had turned to one,
As Castile and Aragon,
Not to be divorced again.

Isabel and Ferdinand:
Two Catholic princes in command,
Two princes with one mighty hand,
Are hailed by the old and newfound land,

By poems, prose, by twangling lutes,
Granada's golden counts and knights,
Sevilla's secret hermeneuts,
Columbus's bold argonauts.

Isabel and Ferdinand
Know no rival for command,
Know only thrones, trains, all that's grand,
Spain's prince, its people, and its land,

Know ships, fish, power, position,
Style, elegance and inquisition,
Blood-judges, seneschals, and mission,
Words, doctrines, tailored definition.

Isabel and Ferdinand
Decide who gets the upper hand,
And who harms whom, how much they stand,
Isabel and Ferdinand.

He who chisels lace from stone,
Rich with tithes, that life is done:
Turbaned or caftaned, it's all one,
Reads the scrolls: an alien!

Hear, princes, hear the exiles cry:
Two long processions stumbling by
Call out to Allah, Adonai,
Call out for mercy to the sky.

And to Gibraltar they have come,
Asia Minor, Byzantium,
The merchant that called Venice home,
Spinoza's light and Rembrandt's gloom.

Isabel and Ferdinand!
Eye of the needle, understand?
One goes through, the other's banned:
In his way a well must stand.

Who learned to love the altar well,
Bowed in Toledo to the bell,
In Goethe's grand abysses fell—
His love's the meaning of that well.

For—Ferdinand and Isabel—
Man needs one homeland, where to dwell;
Milk from your mother's breast will well,
We do not question whence it fell.

For you must dare your new homeland,
Yes, though the milk to poison's turned—
O Isabella, Ferdinand!
Just pay no mind. Just pay no mind.

October 1992

Psalm 137

We sat by the waters of Babylon
And wept. A city cut off from the seas.
Harp on the willow, pain has a new tone:
They need our sweat now, not our agonies,
Nor disputes on our bleeding arteries.
Should I forget you, let my right hand then,
Jerusalem, freeze cold in its amen.

The people scratch our sign upon the wall.
Even their backers know not what they do.
A royal sign, that has survived them all.
Don't blame them, Lord, in their offense to you,
Nor smash their lovely babies on the wall . . . !
And may my mouth spasm in fixity
If I forget you, János Arany.

1992

Mirrorminute

What makes the deer disappear
When love is far away from sight?
Why is the twilight's flaring light
Unseen across the fall of night?

Why won't he stagger any more,
That guard whose life is flickering out?
He only sees what's at his feet,
Anemone's wind-minuet.

Footsteps on the bridge ring out,
Blind darkness beats down everywhere.
The deer will disappear—mark yet
The sky between their antlers clear.

2007

OTTO ORBÁN (1936–2002)

What Is in Schubert's Song?

One flower on the tomb of István Vas

In Schubert's song, in Schubert's melody,
Death, my dear friend, also must surely be.
Its sweetness, then, is sweetness inaccessible,
a deep bitterness, deeply untamable,
the sultan's drop of poison in the crystal by your side,
the shadow standing always at the left hand of the bride
that darkens all the sweet life, all the sweet bygones,
from which the dark Last Judgment still intones
not with its lightning words but the piano's plangency,
the clanging minor chords' wild harmony,
with Schubert's song, with Schubert's melody.

In Schubert's song, in Schubert's resonance,
in every sound death has its residence,
yet to the ear death here has no maleficence:
you're flirting, smiling, twirling at a dance.
Death when it comes in cartfuls is too much of death.
An overdose of Schubert's drug will save your breath.
And shot into a death-world you may roam
by the swift brook where trout swim, the meads in bloom,
and you see deep in a dark wood where there burns a fire
and the Death Maiden's there for your desire
and flame in the lap of music in an eternal trance,
and you shall resurrect, as he on the Third Day once,
In Schubert's song, in Schubert's resonance.

1991

In Which He Supplicates in the Mode of Balassi

God's open firmament,
bird-squadrons turbulent,
free windblown shining light—
brightest of all to me,
sick unto death, to see
here from the balcony's height,
attentively measuring,
with my eyes following
each flitting swallow in flight.

Young ones, tell me where
there is a place more fair
than a strong body that's whole?
Motion, intention
rejoice in contention,
two brothers with one faith and soul;
and soaring and swinging,
go lightly on winging
as a knife through butter will fall.

Too late, airy freedom, it's true,
I have found words for you
now that you're vanished and done;
what though your sun should rise,
your outer form may blaze,
but inside it's frozen and wan;
for time tells us a lie,
like love in its last sigh,
then brightest when soon to be gone.

I call you, carve my seeing
into discernment of being,
I've paid the price in my life:
lurking senility,
hidden infirmity,

pierce me, a murderer's knife—
grant me, your devotee,
that I may truly see
your limitless limit in strife.

On a frail camp-stool I
sat up there in the sky,
in a cloud-trundling nimbus-skein,
and thus I spoke to him
who fills the summers' brim
he who and where none can explain,
yet in all immanent,
in each petal, in each tint,
in every smile though pale with pain.

1992

GYÖRGY PETRI (1943–2000)

Poem by an Anonymous European Poet, 1955

It fades,
      like the two flags that
every year we set in the plastered iron sconces
over the entrance on holidays;
fading, the world loses its color.

Where did the holidays go?

Under thick dust
in the hot
spaces of the attic, silent,
a disassembled world.

The procession has disappeared.

It changed into screaming
and vanished with the wind.
Instead of the holiday poets
now the wind will speak the poems;
it says: mad dust, shimmering heat
over the concrete plaza.

That we once loved women here: unbelievable.

White-hot
furnaces, stretched cables:
over the era
a faltering present
—sinking dust—is floating.

Above the unfinished buildings:
dizzying empires.

What I believed in
I no longer believe.
But that I believed
I remind myself each day.

And I don't forgive anyone.

Our horrible loneliness
crackles
like rusty tracks in the sun.

(Written in 1955) 1971

Collapse

No, there was no explosion,
only collapse.
Who grinds himself up inside
who deceives himself and deceives others
who terrorizes with illusions
has voicelessly subsided.

Can we still think—

one provoked by doubt from the beginning,
giving up the right to doubt,
the idiotic guard of the putrid bathwater,
of the water
in which a baby had been—
can he think of liberation?

Can he even imagine it, who's seen
human bodies dismembering
softly separating
like after lovemaking,
softer than when our flesh
will flake and fall from our bones?

Only it fell apart so voicelessly:
nails slid softly into a rotten beam,
bricks of mud and dust,
that dry porous construction
submitted, as to the depraved bonds of perversion,
when what sense does it make to resist?—
and the earth is flogged with mines and bombardment.

Absurd condescension
beats on the empty air,
like the rain, the rain, the rain.

No, there was no explosion, just collapse.
so long, so long,
jostling, settles
the wet thick dust.
Or is there nothing but that jostling?
that wet swelling scuffle?

The deconstruction of a world.

1967

Angel

signal: the Star of Hatred
                    suddenly
            appears in the daylight
                    sky

charge: on the Don't-Follow-Me
                    bridge
            I throw away
                    my papers

departure: the houses frozen in moonlight
                    glitter
            the Bat spreads his wings
            leaves behind the irredeemable
                    World

1971

Will You Appear?

How crystalline this pure dawn sky!
All is as if composed in space
by some inspired genius, by
some transubstantiating grace.

The dawn redeems this rust-gnawed grille,
the sun is blazing clear and strong,
and resonating to its trill,
the crumbing stucco joins the song.

Thus I in outworn mode began
my poem, my day—and I can't say
how far I'll get, want to, or can.
And you, will you appear halfway?

As usual, coward, I would dodge.
I hope this antiquated span,
this comfortable measured trudge
may help at least to make it scan.

Or better—dear Lord!—should I say,
I'm rocking in its melody?
Long have my ears preserved its way,
heard as if through eternity.

Perhaps it may sweep or wash away
this squeezing thing, I know not what,
that has not left me day on day,
leaping in shock from chest to gut;

Perhaps it will dissolve, undo,
even perhaps come out with it—
So sing out, ancient music, who
thus match the sunblaze opposite!

How long it's been, how long I've yearned
to lose myself, in you to dwell,
exchange my cumbrous being, and
melt in the immaterial.

Since you've been stuck in me, you shy
and hesitant forbidden love,
each side of me, each sharp-crossed I,
has woken to its other half.

Still the sun beams. As old poems say,
the dawn, so crystalline and clear,
waves back—and, heavenly grace, this day
are you too going to appear?

1982–1985

Remembering Our Song

Leaf-litter, chapel, far-off hill,
A windswept melancholy day.
The past cannot be past until
The past must first have passed away.

To find it one must wait, a thing
Mummified, wrapped against decay,
Four or five months until the spring—

*

Four or five years won't bring it on
For you're not here and I am gone
Both of us here and now, I'd find
That such huge light would strike me blind.

Lucky the sun's begun to set
Upon the water darkens yet—
No more   No where
      Never again
That windswept melancholy rain.

1982–1985

KRISZTINA TÓTH (1967–)

Star-meadow

I.

The tearful woman in a negligee
comes out to you, barefoot, stands there alone;
It makes no sense to stay awake this way,
go back to sleep, you say, from today on
it will be different; the crickets cry;
you're on the bench, she has been sleeping with you
twenty years, she whispers, this July;
the summer is too hot, there's a moon-shadow,
and I sleep in my dreams' chaotic voices
and listen, blanketless, to hear whatever
final word the tearful woman chooses
while pulling the mosquito-net together.
A guelder-rose, a guelder-rose! you say
—and you reach down, to turn it to the air,
but now in fragile flakes it breaks away:
the grass is full of fatal petals there.

II.

Everything's linked with secret vein and tendril,
the morning glory runs, cranes to look out,
listens into silence with its blue funnel,
how many more years, then, have you still got?
The handsome bulrush leans against the fence,
a lanky fellow with a cigarette;
it's growing cold, the stars burn on, intense,
the dew-touched grass is starting to get wet;
the bear-paw, though, as if somehow aware,
has thrown off all its leathern leaves; in heaven
the Great Bear isn't going anywhere;
sleep now, for every promise is forgiven—

... it's hard to catch the moment of the morning,
the lightening, but still the moonlight falls:
your body throws two shadows in that dawning,
and each one reaches after different calls.

III.
How still it's got, the crickets now are dumb:
the scent of the gardenias floats out wide.
The hour when one lies awake has come,
and gone, you'll need to get up, go inside;
you'll stop there at the terrace, pinching out
the dried seed-heads, and look the garden over:
the grass looks threadbare, and you are in doubt
where to begin, you see that you could never
tear out the moss, the garden path is full
of it; the sunny parts are overrun
with starwort, by midsummer it will all
be naked, burned, and shriveled by the sun.
Don't bother, just lie back, you tell him; he,
mightily yawning, says *you're blithering,*
this patch is flourishing, why, don't you see
that the star-meadow covers everything?!

1997–2001

Snowdust

How did thirty-two go flitting?
—days and weeks slipped by unwitting?
All through,
past due,

no more credit from the present.
All the present I've been absent,
so passed
the past,

so much time, too much already.
Other wonders were my study:
moonlight,
sunlight

swaddled warm my life's slow waning—
what I've not done, I'm still planning,
my life
now half

done; I guard my face and try
to keep my figure, my
titty
pretty.

Now I've even got a cubby,
(sweet!) who will this winter, maybe,
utter
chatter;

What did they add up to though,
all those years of dusted snow?
Snow-name,
no-name.

Where were they all whirled and scattered,
what, in hearts and words, still mattered,
traceless,
faceless?

Where at last will it all settle—
will *this* live, this jot and tittle?
or through
and through

this snowblind life will I come to

the place at last some day
where I can see
what I may be?!

2000–2003

Essays

The Power of Poetry in the Hungarian Literary Tradition

ZSUZSANNA OZSVÁTH

The sustained effusion of pure verbal energy characterizing Hungarian poetry may be regarded as one of the most striking components of Hungarian culture. Its history goes far back in time. More than eight hundred years ago, under the inspiration of classical and medieval Latin poetry, Hungarian poets began to craft a rich chain of poetic designs, much of it in response to the country's cataclysmic history. With precision, depth, and intensity, these verses give account of their authors' visions of themselves as participants in history and their most personal experiences in the world.

The roots of Hungarian poetry reach further back, however, than the Latin influence that inspired its development. Incorporating the myths and songs of the ancient Magyars, these roots spring from a Finno-Ugric linguistic background and a series of cultural encounters with a wide variety of tribes migrating in the second half of the first millennium from western Siberia to their present location in Central Europe. Subjugating the nomadic immigrants of the sparsely inhabited central plains, at first some of these Magyar groups lived in tribal organizations. They also roamed over the land of other peoples settled in neighboring countries and fought against them. In the tenth century, however, essential changes took place. The Magyars came under Christian influence and formed a kingdom, headed by István I (997–1038). By then, their culture and language surpassed those of their ancestors, whom they had left behind in the foothills of the Urals five hundred years before. Having had numerous encounters with a variety of different people and cultures, the European Hungarians experienced vital clashes between their own and other traditions and changed in the process some of their customs, words, and speech habits.[1] In this way, major linguistic transformations occurred: the tongue of the Magyars amalgamated its Asian roots with European sounds and speech patterns, starting a process that prepared the language for the Latin influence.

The earliest Hungarian literary texts come from the eleventh century. These were religious texts, composed in Latin, using Roman characters instead of the ancient runic writing. Around 1200, further changes took place: religious Latin writings started to be translated into Hungarian. Although, with the expansion of literacy, these translations grew in volume and significance, they never suppressed the ancient popular Magyar folk songs and sagas but rather coexisted with them. In the fourteenth century, secular literature started to develop in the country, taking its impetus from the literary structures, rhyme, and meter of Western poetry.

Politically, too, Hungary attempted to grow along the path of the Western Christian feudal structure. But after István I died, wars and pagan rebellions became recurrent in the kingdom. In addition, inner power struggles and royal disputes interfered with the peaceful consolidation attempts of earlier periods. The ongoing turmoil notwithstanding, the political unity of the Hungarian kingdom remained unchanged until the Mongol invasion (1241–1242). This event altered the country forever. Killing half its population and destroying much of its natural resources, the Mongol hordes left behind rack and ruin of catastrophic dimensions. The damage they caused and the trauma that followed in their wake tore deep

1. Yet, as Géza Balázs says, "In these exchange contacts, the Hungarian language has taken over a large number of words, but has always adjusted them to its own linguistic system and was thus able to preserve its own individuality." *The Story of Hungarian: A Guide to the Language*, trans. Thomas J. DeKornfeld (Budapest: Corvina, 1997), 116.

into Hungarian life and being: this affected Hungarian political decisions and the national consciousness, and, in the long run, the poetic energies, vision, and imagination of generations of Hungarian poets. Indeed, the memory of the Mongol assault did not fade. As time went by and new armies roamed the land of the Magyars, the memory of that cataclysmic assault merged with the consciousness of new threats of destruction. On the popular level, history turned into tales of struggle and identity chronicled by the country's poets, many of whom played a major role in shaping Hungarian collective memory. Over subsequent centuries, stories of foreign occupations, massacres, and heroic resistance were relived, absorbed, and echoed by countless poems, songs, legends, and myths, projecting Hungary as a land suffering from the attacks of violent invaders, gasping for survival. The more foreign armies overran the kingdom and stripped away its independence, the greater the roles these sagas assumed in the country's cultural memory and the greater their impact became on Hungarian intellectual history and political development. Thus, to read Hungarian poetry over the centuries is to be confronted with an ethos of dramatic anguish and heroic defiance that relies on eyewitness accounts of historical events and that has preserved for ages the memory of the past. It also means considering the heroic role Hungarian poets have played in the country's culture as guardians of language, sources of memory, and heroes of freedom for the past eight centuries. One of the first works of art characterized by this consciousness of devastation and by the urge to remember what happened is Master Rogerius's rhythmical prose piece, *Carmen Miserabile* (1243–1244), recalling the Mongol attack that nearly annihilated the nation.

Although the Mongol hordes left after a year, peace did not follow in their wake. In fact, new upheavals began. The tension was aggravated by two factors: the rise of a powerful oligarchy and, in 1301, the sudden end of the bloodline of the ancient Hungarian royal dynasty. Yet curiously enough, despite infighting and hostile disputes, the country did not fall apart. With a new French-Hungarian dynasty taking over the royal succession, Hungary showed signs of recovery, both political and economic. Still, the damage caused by the Mongol destruction had long-lasting consequences. Hungary's foreign trade stagnated, and the country's social structure remained backward for centuries after.[2] As a result, despite its formidable geographical size and powerful historical past, Hungary could not reach the level of progress it needed to thrive and grow—even in the course of two centuries following the Mongol invasion. Its improvements in administration and law, sweeping accomplishments in the realm of culture under the reign of Matthias I Corvinus notwithstanding, the Hungarian kingdom remained vulnerable; and after Matthias's death (1490), it was open to assault.

And this was the worst of times to be defenseless. For just then, at the end of the 1400s, the newly expanding Ottoman Empire started to cast its shadow over the world, threatening those nearby, especially the weak and the unprepared. Working their way up from Asia Minor, Turkish troops defeated the Serbs, reaching the border of the Hungarian kingdom by the middle of the fifteenth century. In the first series of battles, the Hungarians defeated the Ottomans. But the continuous struggle among the various factions of Hungarian magnates and a major peasant revolt in 1514 undermined the strength of the country. With its deteriorating southern defense system unimproved, Hungary became open to foreign attack. In vain did the nobility entreat Rome and Western Europe: help did not come. When the sultan's armies launched a massive attack on Hungary in 1526, they were significantly stronger than their Hungarian counterparts. Defeating and killing virtually all the troops of the Magyars, the Turks also eradicated large numbers of the Hungarian aristocracy in addition to most of the country's high-ranking clergy in the Battle of Mohács. The fleeing Hungarian king, Louis II, drowned in a creek. His death opened the door to the Ottomans.

The dynastic crisis following his death culminated in the Hungarian estates electing two kings to the Hungarian throne: János Zápolyai of Transylvania and Ferdinand I, the Hapsburg archduke and Bohemian king. It was during these rulers' power struggle that the sultan solidified

2. Paul Engel, "The Age of the Angevines, 1301–1382," in *A History of Hungary*, ed. Peter F. Sugar, Peter Hanak, and Tibor Frank (Bloomington: Indiana University Press, 1990), 42–43.

Ottoman rule over Hungary, which lasted for the next hundred and fifty years. He divided the country into three parts: the central and southern section, which came under Ottoman rule; the smaller, western part, assigned to Ferdinand of Austria; and Transylvania, which became an autonomous principality. This "tri-section" had major consequences: it stripped the Hungarian kingdom of its age-old unity and independence, curtailing the country's political development and growth and determining its fate for subsequent centuries.

Still, despite political setbacks, defeats, and destruction, Hungary showed significant signs of progress in the cultural arena during the time span of nearly three hundred years between the Mongol invasion (1241) and the Turkish occupation (1526). One of Europe's first universities was founded in the city of Pécs in the fourteenth century, and in the fifteenth, King Matthias I Corvinus established not only the first Hungarian printing press but also one of Europe's finest libraries, the Bibliotheca Corviniana. At this time, the arts flourished in Hungary as well, with Christian culture expanding on all levels. Latin verse-making developed by leaps and bounds, so much so that it became the form of self-expression of several Hungarian poets. Among these was Janus Pannonius (1434–1472), the humanist poet, renowned across Europe.

But it was not only Latin poetic culture that flourished. Vernacular songs, both old and new, had become highly popular, especially songs about love and patriotism, demonstrating both the broadly based, powerful weave of tradition and new, intricate artistic developments. At the end of the fifteenth century, songs in Latin bewailing the national catastrophes emerged—in addition to a number of beautifully composed, bilingual works—among them, poems about King Saint László and King Matthias that used secular styles, varied imagery, and alliteration. In the sixteenth century, besides religious literature, drama, and love songs, the chronicler's song became popular. Its masters were Sebestyén Tinódi (1505–1556), the songwriter and scrivener of one of Hungary's leading noblemen, Bálint Török, and Péter Ilosvai Selymes, who raised the "wanderer's song" to the level of high poetry. At the same time, Gáspár Károlyi's masterful translation of the Bible came out, which had a significant impact on the development of the language and literature of the Magyars.

When the poets Bálint Balassi (1554–1594) and Miklós Zrínyi (1620–1664) appeared on the scene, the country was still occupied by the Ottomans. Nonetheless, it already had an array of significant poets, both religious and secular. Balassi emerged from their ranks with a volume of new, beautiful poetry. Extraordinary musicality and exceptional range mark his religious songs and passionate courtly love poetry, which shaped the future of Hungarian verse making. Before him, poetry was composed as a text to be sung; in his hands, it became a word construct of poetic expression and meter, changing "the singing culture of the Middle Ages into the lyrical poem of modern times."[3]

Still, Balassi could not withdraw from the world and dedicate himself to verse making alone. His life, like the lives of so many great Hungarian poets over the ages, became part of his country's tragic history. Beginning his military career in 1575, he participated in Hungary's struggle against the Ottoman army and became both an heir to, and a voice of, the Hungarian heroic literary tradition that expected its poets to fight and, if need be, die for their country's independence. Balassi's soldier songs are composed in this spirit, but his life, too, would follow the sacred pattern of self-sacrifice. Like his English counterpart, Sir Philip Sidney, Balassi died in battle, succumbing to the wounds he suffered in defense of his country.

The other poet who was born and came of age during the Ottoman occupation was the poet and statesman Miklós Zrínyi, who for years led Hungary's struggle against the Turks. A national leader and chief of the military forces, Zrínyi was also an opponent of the Hapsburg rule over his country. As a result, he fought passionately for Hungarian freedom and cultural unity, on the battlefield and in political life as well as in the realm of literature. With the first long narrative poem of the country, *Szigeti veszedelem* (The Peril of Sziget), in 1646, an impressive canvas of the battle with the Turks, Zrínyi had a major impact on the development of Hungarian epic literature. At the same time, with the rise of Protestantism and

3. Tibor Komlovszki, "Utószó" (Epilogue), in *Janus Pannonius és Balassi Bálint válogatott költeményei* (Selected Poems of Janus Pannonius and Bálint Balassi), *A magyar költészet kincsestára* (The Goldmine of Hungarian Poetry) (Budapest: Unikornis Kiadó, 1994), 266.

the religious wars, Hungarian thought and art underwent a great variety of experiments. A large number of poets and writers emerged. Among them was the rhetorician of the Counter-Reformation, Péter Pázmány (1570–1637), who became instrumental in developing the national literary language of the Hungarians. Besides the Counter-Reformation, Christian humanist movements flourished, amalgamating with new European ideas, comprising Encyclopedist ambitions, Puritanism, and Pietism. A number of representatives of Hungary's literary tradition cultivated and contributed to these intellectual streams.

The domination of the Ottoman Empire over the large territories of Central and Southeastern Europe did not remain unchallenged by the rest of the world. Austrian military forces defeated the Turkish army at the end of the seventeenth century. In so doing, the Hapsburgs' power expanded, and their demand for Hungary's submission and obedience intensified. However, this development raised the hackles of such independent noblemen as Ferenc Rákóczy II (1676–1735), prince of Transylvania. Rákóczy became the leader of a peasant revolt that exploded into a national uprising against Austrian rule in 1703. Leading the revolution for years without any outside help, Rákóczy was ultimately defeated and exiled. Then the Hapsburg crown took Hungary once more under its wing, keeping it there for the next hundred and fifty years. Defeated again, the Magyars gave in. At this moment in history, the recurrent attacks against Hungarian nationhood and the absolutist ambitions of the Hapsburgs broke the country's resistance. Tired of occupation, foreign invaders, wars, revolutions, and ill-fated national aspirations, the Hungarians stopped fighting altogether. Even poetry fell silent for a while.

After decades of uncertainty and estrangement from the historical past, however, self-awareness and the hope for a better future returned. Patriotic songs in Latin reemerged in the mid-eighteenth century. Latin satires, educational and popular religious songs, folk songs, verse, and drama, both religious and secular, revived. Over time, with the Enlightenment gaining ground, a highly successful language reform and the rise of general education, literature, philosophy, and the study of history had a significant impact on the Hungarian nobility and gentry, and even upon the upper-middle classes. Central to this development were groups of new poets, among them the popular lyricist and translator Sándor Kisfaludy (1772–1844) and Ferenc Kazinczy (1759–1831), poet and reformer of Hungarian language and literary style. But Kazinczy was also a patriot and a liberal who became deeply interested in the ideas of the French Revolution. The Austrian crown did not tolerate such interest; rather, it suspected of treason all sympathizers with the Revolution. Kazinczy was accused of political conspiracy against the crown, found guilty, and sentenced to death. At this point, the poet gave up all ideological resistance. When his sentence was commuted, he left prison and withdrew from politics. Moving to his country estate, he dedicated himself to art for the rest of his life, writing poetry and translating the dramas of Shakespeare and Goethe.

The first major female poet in Hungary, Kata Szidónia Petrőczy (1662–1708) was as much uprooted and shaken by her country's misfortune as were her male counterparts. Unknown until the nineteenth century, her tragic poems were discovered in a book of songs. Deeply religious, most of them revolve around her husband's ill fate, their tragic marriage, her suffering, and her sense of guilt.

Although a hundred years passed between her birth and that of the poet Dániel Berzsenyi (1776–1836), Austria never ceased to tighten its grip around Hungary; there was no end to the humiliation and threats for those who considered themselves to be Hungarian patriots. But Berzsenyi understood the new political reality; he recoiled from explicit political themes and withdrew into the world of literature. A magician with words and an early romantic, Berzsenyi was also deeply affected by Horace. He introduced classical meter and classical structures to Hungarian verse making. His poems are infused with a strain of deep pessimism, sadness, and a sense of desolation.

A contemporary of Kisfaludy, Kazinczy, and Berzsenyi was the Protestant poet Vitéz Mihály Csokonai (1773–1805), another sympathizer with French revolutionary trends. Deeply influenced by the ideas of Rousseau and the concepts of Hungarian Enlightenment, Csokonai also absorbed and pushed to a new climax the achievements of Latin poetry and the Italian and French Rococo. Reinventing the lyrical sounds and structures of these languages, Csokonai amalgamated them with Hungarian verse forms and Hungarian meter.[4]

By the first decades of the nineteenth century, poetry flourished in Hungary; it also started to carry a new, intense self-consciousness of nationalism. Indeed, inspired by French revolutionary thought, Herder's vision of history and ancient myths as significant manifestations of a people's identity, and the rising national awareness of the ethnic groups populating the country, nationalism started to gain weight and significance in Hungary. While the Hapsburgs still ruled supreme, a growing number of poets and politicians, liberal reformers, and intellectuals gathered, struggling against the Austrian oppression. Their major goal was to push ever more intensely for the emancipation of the Hungarian language, Hungarian education, Hungarian administration, and Hungarian public life. As a result, opposition in the Austrian Diet grew: Hungarian nationalism based on the revolutionary notion of "justice for all" and the memory of Hungary's heroic past demanded changes.

In the first few decades of the nineteenth century, this change made itself felt in literature as well. Among the achievements of a growing number of literati emerged the work of the poet and statesman Ferenc Kölcsey (1790–1838), who composed Hungary's tragic national anthem in 1823, and the work of the poet and dramatist Mihály Vörösmarty (1800–1855), who had an enormous influence on Hungarian national literature. Prosecuted for his participation in the 1848 revolution, Vörösmarty went into hiding and lived with his children in abject misery. But his magnificent love lyrics and the fairy-tale drama *Csongor és Tünde* (Csongor and Tünde) manifestly place him among the greatest in Hungarian poetry. József Katona

4. The successful assimilation of the classical forms has become one of the most amazing achievements in Hungarian poetry. As Győző Ferencz claims, Hungarian is "eminently suitable for reproducing the metrical forms of the Greek and Latin tradition." "Language, Politics and Poetic Voice in Contemporary Hungarian Poetry," *Poetry Wales* 37, no. 4 (2002): 57–58. Paul Ignotus observes, "By the beginning of the nineteenth century, Greco-Latin verse forms had become the main vehicle for what the literate Hungarian audience felt was most important to be said." *Hungary* (New York: Praeger, 1972), 308.

(1791–1830) is another author of the time, who wrote *Bánk Bán*, the first Hungarian play for the national theater, as is Imre Madách (1823–1864), whose long historical-philosophical poem *Az ember tragédiája* (The Tragedy of Humankind) is one of the most important dramatic-lyrical achievements in Hungarian literature.

Despite the impressive performance in the country's cultural terrain, Hungary languished politically. It was wounded by the Austrian oppression. Small wonder that when the concept of a unified nation-state became the focus of political and cultural activism in a number of European countries, more and more Hungarians dared to believe in the possibility of restoring Hungary's independence. At the same time, a new generation of Hungarian poets, their gaze fixed on France, became involved in the preparation for revolution. Among them rose to fame the twenty-three-year-old poet Sándor Petőfi (1823–1849), who in 1846 organized with his friends a club for writers, "The Society of Ten." Identifying themselves as "Young Hungary," they composed pamphlets, speeches, poems, and statements pressing for the revolution. When, in March 1848, the revolutionary enthusiasm in Paris reached Vienna and challenged the central authority of the crown, young Petőfi and his group in Budapest rose up against Austrian censorship. They also demanded freedom and independence. This was followed by a set of fresh decrees created by a group of young politicians for a new, independent Hungary. They enacted essential internal reforms and reorganized the parliament. Creating a new leadership as well as disregarding Vienna's objections to change, the Hungarian leader of the revolution, Lajos Kossuth, proclaimed independence from Austria in April 1849. The young Austrian emperor Franz Joseph responded to the challenge by asking the Russian czar, Nicholas I, to intervene. Nicholas arrived with an army of fifty thousand Russian troops. As soon as the Hungarian armies were obliterated, Austria expressed its outrage in the form of savage reprisals. The War of Independence had come to a sudden end; Hungary was forced back under Austrian rule.

Petőfi's voice had a lasting impact, however, on the development of the country's national consciousness and on Hungarian poetry. Blurring the boundaries between popular and high culture, his verses resound in the simple language of ordinary Hungarians. This simplicity is deceptive, however. While Petőfi's lyrics echo the phrasing of Romantic ideas and feelings, and render them in European sounds, styles, and meter, they also resound with the melodic line of the ancient Hungarian folk song, touching upon the deepest layers of the Magyar national memory. Small wonder that every Hungarian knows about Petőfi's self-sacrifice. He volunteered in the army in 1849 and was determined to defend his country against its oppressors. He could not achieve this, however, because Austria won and the Magyars lost the War of Independence. Petőfi died at the age of twenty-six, in the Battle of Segesvár.

Still, the memory of Petőfi and the Romantic revolutionary experience of Hungarian patriotism were not as easily defeated as the small army of the Magyars struggling against their Russian-Austrian conquerors. Intertwining with earlier memories of defeat and resistance, a new sense of remembrance of the recent past reinforced the nation's sense of identity. Petőfi's poet colleague and friend János Arany (1817–1882) was also shaped by the revolution. He earned his reputation with a long and irresistibly moving national epic, *Toldi* (1847–1854), showing a highly complex constellation of passionate, imaginative, and intellectual energies. Set in the fourteenth century, the piece achieved immediate popular acclaim. Besides *Toldi*, Arany composed a large volume of evocative lyric and dramatic poetry. Considered by most as the country's greatest epic poet, author of a number of tragic, beautiful ballads, he also translated into Hungarian works by Shakespeare, Donne, and Keats. But achieving the highest national appreciation did not save Arany from severe depression. Hurt by the ill fate of his country, the defeated revolution, his friend Petőfi's tragic death, and by personal problems, he became disconsolate and bitter. Still, he composed poetry until the end.

In the years following the revolution and Hungary's defeat in the War of Independence, Central Europe started to undergo significant political changes. In the mid-1860s, after hundreds of years of rejections, Hungary suddenly experienced essential modifications in its relationship with Vienna. Due to heavy political losses, Austria was ready to make concessions, letting Hungary become an equal partner to the crown. The

Ausgleich ("Compromise") of 1867 signified the establishment of the dual monarchy Austria-Hungary. From that point until the outbreak of World War I (1914), industry, technology, academic life, and culture grew by leaps and bounds in the Hungarian kingdom. The country flourished, becoming stronger and more prosperous every year. Its capital, Budapest, was the fastest-growing city in Europe by the end of nineteenth century.[5] Even the country's archaic social structures started to change.

In the realm of poetry, new talents appeared. Among them were the fin-de-siècle poets János Vajda (1827–1897), whose visionary images present some of the most impressive achievements of Hungarian poetry, and József Kiss (1843–1921), whose lyrical output and new approaches would become instrumental in bringing modernism to Hungarian poetry. Kiss was editor of the journal *Hét* (Week; 1890–1924), which played a major role in Hungarian culture: it gave the country's rapidly growing, well-educated bourgeoisie a new, intellectual direction.

The last quarter of the nineteenth century seemed to produce an unprecedented outpouring of artistic energy. Beside major poets, such writers as Zsigmond Móricz, Gyula Krúdy, Géza Csáth, and Lajos Nagy appeared, in addition to painters like Tivadar Csontváry and József Ripple-Rónay. Among this group were major artists of both the Hungarian and European avant-garde: János Mattis Teutsch, Lajos Kassák, and László Moholy-Nagy. Also epitomizing the amazing quantity and quality of artists born at this time were the composers Béla Bartók and Zoltán Kodály, Leó Weiner and Ernő Dohnányi. Their styles and approaches reflected and inspired every stream of art at the beginning of the twentieth century, leading to enormous discoveries and changes, and determining the major branches of development for subsequent decades.

At the same time, new genres of Budapest culture flowered. Significant among them was the development of the Hungarian cabaret. Inspired by the French cabaret tradition of comic skits, political and social satire, musical and literary art, Jenő Heltai (1871–1957), novelist, playwright, and

5. See William O. McCagg Jr., *Jewish Nobles and Geniuses in Modern Hungary*, East European Monographs (New York: Columbia University Press, 1972), 31.

lyricist, initiated what has become an important expression of Budapest culture: chanson poetry. This genre shows the influence of the poets of Paris's Latin Quarter, but it also specifically captures the atmosphere of Budapest: its world, its melancholy, and its humor.

The journal *Nyugat* (West; 1908–1941) was the center around which the Hungarian modernist poets grouped themselves. For thirty-three years, it reflected the development of the country's literary achievement. Showcasing the artistic and intellectual innovations of generations of writers and poets and such literary movements as symbolism, expressionism, abstraction, and modernism, *Nyugat* became a depository of the country's intellectual and artistic discourse.

Endre Ady (1877–1919) wrote for *Nyugat*. In fact, with Babits, Kosztolányi, Juhász, Tóth, Kaffka, and Karinthy, he belonged to the "first generation" of *Nyugat* poets, a group of literati responsible for ushering in modernism. Ady's art played a seminal role in this process, a role that may be compared to that of Baudelaire, Verlaine, and Rimbaud in France, or Ezra Pound and T. S. Eliot in England and the United States. His 1906 work, "The Son of Gog and Magog," opens with a radical question that had a huge influence on the direction of twentieth-century poetry in Hungary: "Shall I break through beyond Dévény / With new songs for new times?" (Dévény is the village in West Hungary where the Danube enters the country.) Can one, should one, *dare* one overthrow the tradition that blocks the way to the new world, and dream of words in the voice of the future? These questions ringing through the first half of the twentieth century stirred up heated discussions between the so-called nationalist and internationalist groups of poets and artists in Hungary, among them the modernists, traditionalists, and classicists, with each seeing itself involved in the struggle not only to formulate new styles but also to save the nation's soul, its future, its art.

Like the work of his French and English counterparts, Ady avoids description; his poetry rather moves in the realm of music and seeks affinity with sculpture. Using hard outlines and precise images, it calls forth new visions and new structures. His lyrical constructions rely on metaphysical fantasy, dramatic struggle, archaic and mythical memory. As his critics agree, he had an almost indefinable, deeply individual talent that combined the most sophisticated contemporary inventions with the tradition at full stretch.

In addition, Ady was preoccupied with radical political thought. His poems were a call to arms against the power of Hungary's landed oligarchy and the restrictions forced upon the country's cowed peasantry, indeed, against a feudal system that had not changed significantly despite the rapid industrialization taking place around the end of the nineteenth century. And when World War I exploded, Ady, in the tradition of the ancient Hungarian poet-prophets, foresaw the catastrophe. He composed impassioned antiwar poetry, warning of destruction.

He could not stop the catastrophe, of course. The storm had started to gather in the nineteenth century, when the country's large ethnic groups—the majority of the monarchy's population—began to question the Magyars' right to rule them and decided to struggle against what they claimed was Hungary's disregard for other people's self-determination. Threatened and polarized, the Magyar leadership hesitated to act. It held to the past, insisting on its privileges. But the tension did not go away; rather, it intensified and became the focus for subsequent destructive developments. And when World War I erupted, Hungarians following the path of Austria and Germany opened themselves up to their country's defeat. Nor could they imagine their own declining role among the great nations of the world. That was their tragedy: not only did Hungary lose the war, with nearly four hundred thousand people dead and over a million wounded; it lost its power and influence in the world. Dictated by the Treaty of Trianon (1920), the country lost two-thirds of its historical territories and one-third of its people to foreign governments. In the meantime, Béla Kun's brutal Communist dictatorship was defeated by the even more brutal counterrevolutionary army of Admiral Horthy (1919), who established a semi-Fascist government and remained in power for the next twenty-five years.

• • •

Shaken and divided throughout the interwar period, Hungarian literary figures attempted to recover after a while, but their differences did not disappear: they became associated with different aesthetic-political groups who passionately opposed one another. Less politically minded than most of her contemporaries, Margit Kaffka (1880–1918) belonged to the group of

Ady's modernist contemporaries. Like her English counterpart Virginia Woolf, Kaffka addressed and wanted to be heard by the "new women" of the twentieth century. Her language is proud, strong, luminous, and creative. Her poems communicate refusal of defeat, expecting nothing but happiness and fulfillment.

Like Kaffka's poems, the lyrics of Gyula Juhász (1883–1937) had a significant impact on the development of Hungarian poetry. Entering the Piarist novitiate after high school, Juhász left the seminary six months later because of his interest in poetry. But he was tortured by guilt throughout his life, deciding to return to the priesthood, again and again breaking his vows. This struggle underlies Juhász's lyrics, manifesting itself in both an almost pagan nostalgia for life and its pleasures and a deep sense of guilt.

Continuing the centuries-old Hungarian poetic tradition of political involvement, Juhász participated in the country's workers' movement and supported the 1918 October Revolution. He was then prosecuted by the Horthy government (Miklós Horthy had been the regent of Hungary during the interwar period) and taken to court for an article he wrote on behalf of the workers. There can be no doubt that his persecution did not help to resolve the dark existential conflicts that had tortured the poet since his youth (although it obviously did not cause them, either). Pessimistic, haunted by guilt, he struggled against them throughout his life. With time, depression took over. After several suicide attempts, he killed himself with an overdose of tranquilizers.

A contemporary of Ady, Kaffka, and Juhász, and one of the major figures shaping the literary epoch was Mihály Babits (1883–1941), editor of *Nyugat* for over a decade. Babits's poems absorbed the styles and modes of writing of the great classical poets as well as the work of nineteenth- and twentieth-century poets such as Mallarmé, Verlaine, Eliot, and Rilke. They also absorbed the new movements of the time: modernism, impressionism, and expressionism. During World War I, Babits was a Catholic pacifist, but he withdrew from politics after the hostilities ended. Attacked by many for his conservative artistic and cultural values during the 1920s and 1930s, he tried to keep himself out of the violent political struggles of the Left and the Right alike. He gave up hope for national unity, but he never abandoned his belief in the redemptive power of poetry.

Another member of this first generation of modernists was Dezső Kosztolányi (1885–1936). Referring to himself as a "Homo aestheticus," Kosztolányi refused to see the role of the poet as confined to a political stance or determined by "political engagement." He saw it in much broader terms. His poems reveal extraordinary sensitivity, dream-like visions of colors and symbols, and a musical perception that recalls Debussy. They merge musicality with spiritual and psychological elements, comparable to the best of Rilke, Georg Trakl, or Elsa Lasker-Schüler.

Árpád Tóth (1886–1928) belonged to the same group of *Nyugat* poets as Babits. His lyrical genius finds its origins in the movements of impressionism and secession, but it also shows the influence of the Pre-Raphaelites. Endowing his poems with a quasi-magical power, Tóth was capable of expressing feelings and perceptions of an ineffable, dream-like existence.

The country's popular humorist, essayist, novelist, short story writer, and poet Frigyes Karinthy (1887–1938) was one of the most interesting and talented men of his time. A satirist who emphasized the absurd elements of daily life, Karinthy made fun of everything: the nature of human relationships, schoolchildren and their status vis-à-vis teachers, national heroes, honor, competitive sports, family life, and politics. Hated by the Rightists and the anti-Semites for poking fun at "country and family," he went on mocking the culture till the end of his life. His poetry shows deep sensitivity and intensity, revealing insights of extraordinary psychic depth.

Among those coming of age outside the dominion of *Nyugat* was Lajos Kassák (1887–1967), poet, writer, and painter, who became a major advocate of the avant-garde in Hungary. Turning against "bourgeois" taste, much of his early poetry is composed in free verse and appears in experimental Dadaist style, suffused by lyrical expressions that show a sharply defined visual focus. At first, he was influenced by futurism and the constructivist styles; but later, he turned more elegiac, more classical. Starting out as an apprentice locksmith, he was influenced by socialist ideas from an early age. During World War I, he not only participated in strikes and demonstrations against the war but in 1915 founded the journal *A Tett* (Action), a publication that opposed the war. Participating in the formation of the revolutionary government in Hungary in 1918, Kassák was prosecuted by the Horthy regime. He left the country in 1919, returned in

1925, and remained in Hungary despite the danger to him under Horthy and, later, of course, under the Communist regime.

Milán Füst (1888–1967), like most major poets of his generation, was a contributor to the literary journal *Nyugat*. But Füst was free of the political-social pressures under which many Hungarian literati of his age lived. Rather than being preoccupied with the problems of the poor and the exploited, Füst wrote about the tragic nature of human life and emerged as one of the great poets, experimental novelists, and dramatists of his time. With his dramatic images, biblical metaphors, and resounding voice, he brought new themes, new sounds, and new phrasing to Hungarian poetry.

The so-called second generation of poets publishing in the journal *Nyugat* arose during the 1920s—among them, Lőrinc Szabó (1900–1957) and Gyula Illyés (1902–1983). Szabó's poetic approach derives from two major sources: late expressionism and, similar to the approach of Arpád Tóth, the style of the Pre-Raphaelites. His expressive, musical poetry revolves around self-analysis and the relationship of the self to the other.

Illyés also plays an important role in the literature of twentieth-century Hungary. Intensely concerned with the fate of the peasants, he composed essays and narrative lyrical poems, too. And while his early lyrics show deep affinities with expressionist and surrealist trends, they also amalgamate the structures and idioms of Hungarian folk poetry. His famous poem "One Sentence about Tyranny," which became known in the country just before the Hungarian Revolution of 1956, had a major impact on Hungary's political development and artistic vision.

More than Kassák, who, despite his conflict with the Hungarian establishment during the 1920s and 1930s, was closely connected with most Left-oriented artist groups and other artists living and working in and outside the world of *Nyugat*, Attila József (1905–1937) was a loner. The child of a Romanian drifter and a Hungarian washerwoman, József added a new resonance to Hungarian speech patterns and new rhythmic combinations, images, and sounds to the traditional lyrical forms of poetry. A shaman-like virtuoso of rhyme and metrics, a master of classicist and modernist approaches and styles, a creator of vision and magical expression, József also used with ease the intellectual-artistic currents of his time. In his early youth, he was a populist. But after a while, he decided to take the side of the radical Left and wrote verses about both the wretched life of the poor and the future rise of common humanity. Of course, such poetry did not delight the defenders of Hungary's semi-Fascist Horthy system. József was treated as a pariah in his country. Later he changed again. He started to see an inherent threat to individual life in the Communist system and turned decisively against it. He noted both its danger and its proximity to Fascism. Undergoing psychoanalysis, he penetrated this process as well and composed some of the deepest, most tender, and moving poetry of the twentieth century about childhood, women, the world, his disappointments, and his naked despair. Hurt, lonely, and bereft of hope, József committed suicide at the age of thirty-two.

The country's poetic production was not destroyed by these losses. Involved in the political turmoil during the 1920s and 1930s, many of Hungary's leading artists and poets felt the need to fight for their nation's survival.[6] They not only became great innovators and artists but also understood their own national significance: their duty and power as poets in the world. Split during World War I over pacifist or pro-war activities, by the 1920s and 1930s, they were polarized by other bitter struggles: by leftist ideology, rightist and anti-Semitic theories, populism, the memory of the country's heroic past and its wounded present, and the threat of the nation's destruction. And there was no time for healing. Although the country made some progress during the second half of the 1920s, by the end of the decade, the Great Depression had paralyzed Hungary's economy and radicalized many a politically engaged young poet. With the rise of Hitler, the country shifted towards the radical Right. The process culminated in World War II and the Holocaust. Together they led to the death of about one million Hungarians. In the war and the battles in the Ukraine, nearly 270,000 Hungarian soldiers died or became prisoners of war; another 150,000 to 200,000 people died in the

6. For the political involvement of Hungarian artists in the first two decades of the twentieth century, see S. A. Mansbach, *Standing in the Tempest: Painters of the Hungarian Avant-Garde, 1908–1930* (Santa Barbara, CA: Santa Barbara Museum of Art, 1991).

siege of Budapest. In the Shoah (starting with earlier attempts at humiliating, exiling, and killing the Jews), 570,000 people perished—among them, thousands of Jewish intellectuals, artists, poets, and musicians. Horthy's rule lasted for twenty-five years, until it was swept away by the Russian army during the last months of World War II.

The poets Miklós Radnóti (1909–1944) and Sándor Weöres (1913–1989) belonged to the "third generation" of *Nyugat* contributors, but their fate and art differed a great deal. Weöres withdrew from the public domain and kept a low profile during the war years and the Holocaust. He composed poetry that put into words the difficult-to-communicate experience of the early self, its poetic presence, musical reverberations, and impact on the mind. In this way, many of his verses recreate a sense of miraculous enchantment that borders on surrealism and mysticism. Exploring a wide range of structure and technique, Weöres composed some of the most important, singularly beautiful lyrics of our time.

Radnóti, on the other hand, was classified as a Jew by the anti-Jewish laws of Nürnberg that were adopted by the Horthy government in 1938, 1939, and 1941. Conscripted three times in the course of three years, he was taken to Yugoslavia during the late spring of 1944 to work for the Germans in Bor, a copper mine. In the autumn of that year, as the German army evacuated the Balkans, Radnóti was taken on a death march back to Hungary. No longer able to walk, he was shot by his Hungarian guards and buried in a mass grave with twenty-one of his comrades.

Young Radnóti started out as an expressionist lyricist whose poems' multicolored images and free-verse patterns early reveal the potential of a great talent. As times changed culturally and politically, however, Radnóti matured, and his vision shifted. He noted the events taking place in Germany—in fact, he became preoccupied with them, foreseeing the impending catastrophe. While he continued to write love poetry throughout his life, his prophetic poems started to revolve around images of calamity and mass death as early as the mid-1930s. Arranged in neoclassicist structures, his late work incorporates the Greek measure as well as the French Alexandrine, the Italian sonnet, the Hungarian folk song, and the meter of the *Nibelungenlied*. While the poems of Radnóti's last years appear in formal classical structures, they create their own melodic lines and project prophetic visions of both his own tragic future and the mass catastrophes that would shake the world.

István Vas (1910–1991) a friend and colleague of Radnóti, survived the Holocaust in Budapest. Starting out as a young poet, he was interested in the works and concepts of the avant-garde, but eventually he returned to the rhyme schemes and classical forms of the Hungarian literary tradition.

The end of World War II and the country's losses, Radnóti's death and the discovery of the mass grave containing his remains, knowledge of the potential global nuclear wasteland, and the undeniable fact of the literal ashes of European humanism shattered deeply held beliefs in the moral power of art and poetry. And when at least some sort of healing could have started, Hungary found itself yet again overseen by "larger," global political interests. Its future was now determined by the decision of the Allies, who gave in to the pressure from Stalin and created a partitioned Europe. After 1948, with the tension intensifying between East and West, Hungary's Communists, led by the Soviets, took over leadership of the government. One would assume that amid such threats and danger, Hungarian poetry could hardly relocate its center, find its own voice or its own tradition. Yet, again and again, it tried.

• • •

While the great established poets, Füst, Illyés, Kassák, and Vas, continued to write and publish poetry during the second half of the twentieth century, several young poets emerged during that time period, trying to cope with the new world. Among the first young poets publishing after World War II, and among those with a major impact on postwar Hungarian poetry, was János Pilinszky (1921–1981). Much of Pilinszky's work revolves around "what happened" and around his awareness of the power of the past. A Catholic poet whose work may yet be defined as denominational, he often speaks directly to God while he also suffers from the lack of divine presence in the world. Drafted into the army in 1944, he was taken to Germany to fight against the Allies. After the war, as a POW, he came across several German concentration camps, among them Ravensbrück. He never forgot this encounter. Several of his major poems reveal the memory of those horrors, giving account of what he saw and experienced.

Ágnes Nemes Nagy (1922–1991) is one of Hungary's major poets of the late twentieth century. She published her first volume of poetry shortly after World War II. During the Rákosi era, however, she was allowed to publish only as a translator and to work only on children's books. Change came after years of silence when, in 1957, the Communist leadership finally agreed to allow the publication of her poetry. As soon as this happened, she became a major inspirational force, determining the path of development of the country's young poets. Displaying a remarkable fusion of "objective lyricism" and "classical modernity," her work is not large in volume, but its dynamic power and amazing creativity have had a huge impact on the new Hungarian lyric scene.

Zsuzsa Beney (1930–2006) also had a great influence on Hungarian lyrics after World War II. Novelist, essayist, and literary critic, she was one of the most original voices in postmodern Hungarian literature. Attempting to transform idea into metaphor, she composed poetry that revolves around life and death, paradoxically manifesting the pleasure and delight embedded in our world of suffering. In addition to the role she played in the realm of the new literature, she worked as a medical doctor (a pulmonologist) and as a professor of literary studies at one of the Hungarian universities, mourning the deaths of her eighteen-month-old baby and her husband for the rest of her life.

Ágnes Gergely (b. 1933) composed a rich body of literary works characterized by a refined poetic taste and the wide-ranging artistic consciousness of the European tradition. Influenced by English poetry, she was especially affected by the work of William Butler Yeats. Having published thirteen volumes of poetry, several novels, many essays, three memoirs, and a wide range of translations, she has been deeply preoccupied by the Hungarian-Jewish conflict, which, while the topic of a few excellent books, has rarely been a subject of open discussion in the mainstream press among the Hungarian literati and public. She, however, is one of those few poets who try to broach the subject again and again. The pain of the murder of her father and the attempts at the cover-up of the country's anti-Semitic past by the Hungarian media, government, and general public rise to the surface in several of her poems. Irony and tragedy underlie her work, which tries to deal poetically with these and other everyday issues, evidence of passionate emotion.

Atrocity and politics shaped the life and poetry of Otto Orbán (1936–2002). His father was murdered by the Hungarian Nazis, and he lived and composed poetry most of his life in Russian-occupied Hungary. He was influenced by modern American lyrics, but he also composed a great variety of poems in other styles, often using postmodern visions. On the one hand, he followed the classical ambitions of the circle of poets writing for the Hungarian literary journal *West* (1908–1941); on the other hand, however, he fused the achievements of the past with the discoveries of the avant-garde. Regarded as one of the greatest poets of his generation, Orbán combined mythical themes and images in his poems with real-life experiences.

György Petri (1943–2000) was both a highly respected poet and a famous translator. He also followed the tradition of earlier Hungarian poets, who opposed the Hungarian political establishment directed by the Soviet Union and the pressure under which the country lived. But the Communist governments of the 1960s and 1970s were not as powerful as they had been before. As a result, they could not completely silence him. Widely read by his numerous followers, partly because he was a great poet, partly because he was a cult figure resisting the system, he published regularly in samizdat. His verses fight against injustice and oppression, amalgamating an ironic yet deeply pessimistic outlook and bitter language, imitating classical literature while using present-day slang. Yet his seemingly contradictory approach is not only restricted to his political fights. It also emerges in his erotic poems, which are often contrasted with emotional detachment.

Szabolcs Várady (b. 1943), a recipient of several major Hungarian literary prizes, including the Graves Prize (1981), the Tibor Déry Prize (1987), the Attila József Prize (1991), and the Palladium Prize (2004), is a well-known poet and translator of American and English poetry, drama, and essays. In his lyrics, he frequently uses such musical devices as rhyme and metrical structures, which he combines with an ironic stance and an object-oriented approach.

Krisztina Tóth (b. 1967) is one of Hungary's most highly esteemed young poets. A winner of several literary prizes, she is a major representative of Hungarian classical modernity. Her poetry shows the rich formal culture of the past but also a sharp vision and the hard abstractions of everyday life. Arising from rich Hungarian and European structural traditions, it combines glimmering, surreal visual elements and ironic-abstract approaches. Many of her poems appear in a mysterious light that is accompanied by critical and intellectual concerns and irony. Tóth also designs and produces stained-glass windows.

• • •

Despite the wars and murderous persecutions suffered by Hungary in the twentieth century, the country's poetic genius never completely left the culture: even in the worst of times, it did not disappear from public life. Dormant for just very short periods, it survived two world wars, the Holocaust, and the Communist terror regimes, constantly experimenting with and cultivating new structures, bursting with new energy, continuing not only to discover ever-changing new worlds but also to recover the legacy of its own tradition.

The "Thou" of Hungarian Poetry

Translator's Note

FREDERICK TURNER

Every great national literature is both unique and representative of humanity's collective literary imagination. Indeed, what we mean by "great" is perhaps precisely the union of these two characteristics. A literature that was not unique, if one could imagine such a thing, might hardly be worth translating, since its qualities would be available elsewhere; a literature that did not contain the spirit of humanity as a whole would be of local interest only, village gossip or arbitrary cult obsession.

In translating these poems, we have been guided by both characteristics of the Hungarian tradition. It is, of course, hard to tease them out from each other, since, as Blake believed, the universal finds its favorite dwelling place in "minute particulars." But the reader might find useful the impressions of a poet-translator who has been close to the material for years, and appreciate the help of a docent, so to speak, who can point to the special passages or compositional gestalt of the paintings in the gallery.

Hungarian poetry is, for instance, more than usually full of personification. Natural objects, emotions, institutions, traditions take on the quality of being a "you" or "thou" rather than an "it," and in a sense every Hungarian poem is an ode, an address to its subject as to one who might speak back, and who perhaps is given the voice to do so in the poem itself. Consider, for instance, the earliest poem in our collection, the folk song

"Spring Wind Makes the Waters Rise," which like any other ode is a second-person direct address and in which the girl addressed is metaphorically a "flower." But it soon becomes clear that the comparison between the human and the natural is not just a metaphor: the tragic human life force is the same as the natural energies of life and death. The winds, streams, and mating birds of nature are the counterparts of the passions of men and women:

> Spring wind makes the waters rise
> My flower, my flower.
>
> Every bird a mate must choose,
> My flower, my flower.
>
> Who then is my choice to be,
> My flower, my flower?
>
> I'll choose you and you'll choose me,
> My flower, my flower.

Thus the ode form is more than a trope but is organic to the poem's meaning; the "thou" of the poem is no more nor less personal than nature itself. Or consider the hapless black-sealed letter from his mistress, which Mihály Csokonai interrogates and harangues with an effect that is full of both pathos and comic self-ridicule; everything comes to life because everything has a will and an inner force:

> Black seal on my truelove's letter,
>   Loose at last what you conceal!
> Show to my sad head your matter;
>   Life, or death, will you reveal?
> Make or break—
> Lord, I shake!
>
> Shake! Perhaps her rose-stem's smitten
>   By a pain that tears her heart,
> Or her grief—or death!—are written
>   In the dead black of your art.

Does she save
Me a grave?

In a grave? or loves another?—
 Hurls me from her heart's demesne,
A death-sentence to her lover?
 That is what the seal must mean.
It's no lie.
I must die.

In Dániel Berzsenyi's "Supplication," even the principles of physics
are personified and give praise to their God:

Zenith and Nadir praise and glorify you.
 The groaning struggle of tempests, the lightning's
  Skyfire, dewdrops, flowers' delicate scapes
   Blazon forth your manifold handiwork.

The many hymns to their country, by poets like Ferenc Kölcsey, Sándor
Petőfi, and Mihály Vörösmarty, invariably speak to it as to a person; in János
Arany's poem, the crow is not just metaphorically a witch and the bardic
tradition of Wales is a living presence that cannot be killed by eliminating
its members; József Kiss's white cloud is the watching face of God; Margit
Kaffka sees her little boy's "minikin booties" as animate in themselves; the
Danube speaks in person to Endre Ady and to Attila József; Lajos Kassák's
heroic technology is the expressed intention of the people; Mihály Babits's
spring and winter are intentional forces of creation and destruction; Miklós
Radnóti's angel looks out from tree and season and even electric cable; and
the starry morning sky of Dezső Kosztolányi becomes a dance floor full of
divine beings. The personification can be comic, as in Frigyes Karinthy's
outrageously funny "Dandelion," where the poet's relatives are the winds:

My father was Mr. Howling Storm—and my mother the
 celebrated Ms. Typhoon of Arkansaw.
Then there's my brother-in-law, Funnel Cloud—
Dandelion-fluff, haven't you ever tangled and swirled aswoon
On the spin-crest of the cloud-piercing whirlwind?

Or it can be tragic, as in József's stunted industrial landscapes, where the material detritus of technology takes on a sense of personal desolation. Even in the exhausted despair and terminal inauthenticity of the last days of Soviet communism, in the darkest poems of Gyula Illyés, István Vas, and György Petri, the world is still personified and addressed. Illyés makes tyranny itself a sort of person; Vas addresses the human mind and thanks the great dead authors he is translating so subversively; and for Petri, in a world where all significance and spirit has been leached out by lies, the dust and the loneliness themselves become active intentionalities.

One could well argue that all poetic traditions contain some version of personification, and one could give examples like Keats's odes or the animate landscapes of Homer, Horace, and Virgil, or the violent subjectivizing of all the "symboles" in the "forêt" of the French symbolist movement; one could cite the English metaphysicals or Dante or Lorca or Schiller as great personifiers. But in Hungarian poetry *every* poem personifies and subjectifies its material in some way or another; personification is not just another trope or technique but is in a sense the principle of the poetry, a giving voice to the voiceless-but-sentient spirits that inhabit nature and culture.

But is not this "giving voice" itself one of the special functions of poetry—so that it extends the franchise, so to speak, the vote in the constitution of reality as we accept it, from human beings to trees and valleys and cities and cultural "memes"? In this, I think, Hungarian poetry in its uniqueness reveals to us, paradoxically, something about all human poetry—that in a sense all poetry strains toward the ode, all poetry insists that the universe is alive and its components are aware and acting freely. Hungary is one of the leading scientific nations; for its size it has contributed a disproportionate share to the human understanding of nature, and its science is more than usually full of a kind of "Einfühlung," in Goethe's term, an empathy with what it studies. Is this a distant inheritance from the ancient Magyar shamanic tradition, with its animist and pantheist origins? Do scientific and poetic insights perhaps come from the same place? As one might say that all English poetry is in some sense dramatic, and in this uniqueness reveals more clearly than elsewhere the essential dramatic trading that must go on in all good poetry; or that all German poetry is based on a sort of fairy tale in which the novice learns wisdom, and thus tells us something about another function of poetry in general; or that all Chinese poetry raises its eyes from the immediate view of the midnight river or mossy tree to the vast and melancholy vision of "ten thousand *li*," and thus reflects a hidden theme in all other poetry—so Hungarian poetry reveals the universal in its particularity.

The deep theme of personification in Hungarian poetry also serves as a guide for the translator. Just as the Hungarian poet gives to his or her material the dignity of being a "thou," so the translator, in all fairness, must do the same for the poem itself. The poem cannot be for us a "text" in the postmodernist, poststructuralist sense; the author cannot be an "author function." Neither poem nor author should be forced to lie supine beneath the critical knife of the translator. Certainly the translator must also be a consummate critic—but such criticism must be a form of communion with the poet, a communion that is humble and utterly respectful. If the translator fails to honor the generous contract implicitly offered by the poet (I will count everything as a thou: will you, in response, treat me as a thou as well?), the translation falls, as Jonathan Swift put it, "like a dead bird of paradise to the ground." Zsuzsanna Ozsváth and I found ourselves again and again compelled to follow with love and respect the inner moves of the poet's mind. At times I, the ignorant instrument, knowing only a few words of Hungarian, could guess at the meaning of the next few lines, so perfectly had Zsuzsi rendered the subjective meaning of the poet's imagery and cadence.

There was indeed a deeper "move," too, in Hungarian poetry, one that the "new historicism" has tried, largely without success, to capture: the movement of European consciousness and feeling, the whole western world slowly thinking itself out through billions of conversations and dozens of generations. That too must be taken as a kind of "thou," or even as a "we." Hungarian poetry is both a fresh, wild, Asiatic response to European literature and culture, and at the same time an epitome of European sensibility, a concentrated crystal of all that was going on in the mind of the continent. Bálint Balassi, for example, is clearly of the same Weltanschauung as Philip Sidney, his contemporary, with the same mixture of martial elegance, vaulting courage, hyperbolic love of the lady, and ironic but helpless awareness of his own absurdity in loving:

With thy love my heart's afire,
Thou, the princess of my prayer,
Heart and soul and love entire,
Hail, my soul's one last desire!

Finding Julia I, enchanted,
Greeted her as here presented,
Bowed in reverence unwonted,
But a smile was all she granted.

Csokonai's exquisite love poetry reminds us of Fragonard and Mozart and those white and gold rococo plaster ceilings painted with nymphs and glowing flowers:

Piping philomelas!
Dream-tints in the eye!
Pleasures! Hopes! Sweet Lillas!
Good-bye, good-bye, good-bye!

In Petőfi, we hear the authentic nobility of Beethoven's *Eroica* and *Fidelio*, the fierce hope for liberty unleashed all over Europe by the French Revolution (and so bitterly disappointed by its outcome):

Across my corse
The snorting horse
In squadrons gallop to their hard-won victory
And leave me trampled by the charging cavalry.—
There let them gather up my scattered bones
And with a sad, slow music's solemn tones
Let them observe the day of burial,
And under banners veiled in funeral
Devote their heroes to a common grave
Who died, world liberty, thy name to save!

In Arany, we recognize the same impulse that inspired poets like Coleridge and Hardy to turn to the ancient narrative ballad form (and Arany is as important a poet, I think, as either):

Fish, flesh, and fowl, all under sky
Pleasing and sweet I see;
But yet methinks the devil slinks
In these lords' courtesy.

Gentles, gentles! you wretched dogs!
Who'll sing King Edward's tales?
Where is the guest who'll toast my geste—
Bring forth the bard of Wales!

Ady represents the whole continent in its modernist turn when he swears to sing the new songs, when he claims the future for a new voice compounded of French beauty and Magyar vigor:

Fear not, my ship, for you carry Tomorrow,
The drunken oarsman they jeer at, the hero.
Fly, my brave ship,
Fear not, my ship, for you carry Tomorrow.

In József and Radnóti, the twentieth century itself speaks, with its industrial landscapes, its struggle of bloody ideologies, its immense hopes for freedom, justice, and equality, its shocking disappointments. Here is József, his proletarian visionary symbolism at its most intense:

The warehouse is a shipwrecked bark,
the foundry's an iron barge: behold
the foundryman dreams through the mold
a scarlet babe of molten gold.

But he also records his deep misgivings about all ideologies, right or left, with an ambivalence that is the only honorable and humane response to the atrocities of the twentieth century:

We've laid poor Kosztolányi in the mire,
and on mankind, as cancer did on him,
horrible monster-states gnaw limb by limb,
and we, aghast, ask what's the next disease,

whence fall new wolvish ideologies,
what newer poison boils within our blood—
how long, and where, you can still read aloud? . . .
. . . .
Sit down. Start our favorite story—please.
We'll listen; happy he who only sees
your face among our race of evil will,
to know there's one true European still.

And here is Radnóti, in a poem that sums up the surreal terror of the
whole period:

The moon sways in a foamy sky.
How strange that I'm alive. A bland,
efficient death searches this age
and they turn white on whom it lays its hand.

Sometimes the year looks round and shrieks,
looks round and faints away.
What kind of autumn lies in wait,
what winter dulled with agony to grey?

The forest bled, and every hour
in that revolving time bled too.
The wind was scrawling numbers, huge
and darkening in the unsettled snow.

More succinctly, perhaps, than any of the European existentialists, Milán
Fűst outlines the philosophical and moral predicament that nineteenth-
century scientific materialism and positivism had bequeathed to us:

Dark and frigid the earth. And it will be chillier still, you'll see,
    as in slow measure it turns
Slanting toward Orion's foggy projection. Touch its lumps: they
    too are dusty and chill.
And imagine: everything's going to be dustier: forever greyer
    will be the world—as if the cold

Were to permeate, pierce the essence of things, and the dust here,
    too,
Prevail forever . . .

The burst of female imagination that became public after the second world war, in response to the collapse of the phallic dictatorships, is represented with astonishing originality by Ágnes Nemes Nagy, Zsuzsa Beney, Ágnes Gergely, and Krisztina Tóth. And the spiritual revulsion against positivism and materialism, which gathered force in Europe in the wake of the collapse of the great secular ideologies, is passionately exemplified by János Pilinszky, Otto Orbán, and Szabolcs Várady—and always, of course, in the second-person form of address.

With each age there comes a new diction, a new vocabulary, a fresh burst of emotions and moods, a revised underpinning of philosophical reason and scientific knowledge. In our translations, we have tried to be guided by that European mind, too, as well as by the poet's blazing spark of it. So we have attempted faithfully to reflect the language and tone of the times of the poems, unafraid of archaism and inversion in modern English terms if they echo the temporal oddness of old Hungarian poetry, but of course avoiding them in modern writers (unless the writers themselves bend their diction to the archaic for some ironic or nostalgic purpose). Likewise, we have avoided modern ideas and language when translating older poets—no punk-rock performances of Shakespeare, so to speak.

We have also followed our tested translation practice of reproducing in English the meter, cadence, rhyme scheme, and stanzaic structure of our originals. For the "thou" of the poet is never more intimately incarnated than in the rise and fall of his or her voice, characteristic emphasis, and unique poetic music—in the breath pattern, the pauses, the flow or staccato of personal address. And meter, because it provides a rhythmic yardstick against which such idiosyncrasies can be precisely calibrated, acts as the medium for the resurrection of that voice in another language. Together with its emphatic highlighting of rhyme, meter is a reliable guide for the translator—it is a Virgil, so to speak, who can lead the timid Dante into the underworld or overworld of a foreign dead poet's imagination, and conduct him safely back out again into the ordinary daylight of his own language; or perhaps, in a more exact metaphor, it is the lyre with which the Orpheus-translator is enabled to open the gates of the land of the dead.

The Hungarian poets are almost without exception virtuosos in the arts of meter. Bálint Balassi was already in the sixteenth century devising elaborate, internally rhymed stanzas, crafted to fit the notes of a song:

> Scarlet the guidons, bright heraldry gladdens
> > on surcoat and standard below,
> In the vanguard he races, the field's vast spaces
> > courses, like wild winds that blow;
> Gaily caparisoned, bright helms all garrisoned,
> > plumed in their beauty they go.
>
> On Saracen stallions they prance in battalions,
> > hearing the blast of the horn,
> While those who stood guard when the night watch was hard,
> > dismounted, rest in the dawn:
> In skirmish and night-fray unending well might they
> > with watching be wearied and worn.
>
> For the fame, for good name, and for honor's acclaim,
> > they leave the world's joys behind,
> Flower of humanity, pattern of chivalry,
> > to all, the pure form of high mind;
> And as falcons they soar over fields of grim war,
> > unleashed to strike in the wind.

Csokonai constructs ingenious nonce stanzas to convey the precise shape of his feeling, as for instance in his ode "To Hope":

> Ah, but my fresh roses
> Withered all away;
> Springs and greeny closes
> Turned to sere and grey;
> All my springtime madness

Winter grief now stings;
That old world of gladness
Flew on worthless wings.
If but Lilla you had left me
I should feel no wrong;
No complaint that you bereft me
Should weigh down my song.
In her arms those sorrows
I could all forget,
Pearl wreaths, glad tomorrows,
I should not regret.

Here eight trochaic trimeters with alternating feminine and masculine endings are succeeded by two pairs of alternating trochaic feminine tetrameters and masculine trimeters, and concluded by four alternating trimeters; the whole is rhymed ABABCDCDEFEFGHGH. Two pairs of feminine and masculine lines are rhymed with each other to make a double antithesis, which is then balanced against a second four-line group, contrasted with a third four-line group with the tetrameter variation at lines 9 and 11, and reechoed in a final four-line group that returns to the form of the first in a truly musical fashion. The sixteen-line stanza is now antithetically doubled against a second identical stanza, and this pair of stanzas balanced by a second pair, to make sixty-four lines, or two to the sixth power. In meaning, the whole poem is a pattern of antithetical contrasts, between male and female, despair and hope, winter and spring, darkness and light, absence and presence. The result is an exquisite and airy confection whose inner form is utterly musical, and which, despite the exact precision of its construction, is full of life and movement.

Dániel Berzsenyi and, two centuries later, Miklós Radnóti go to the rich heritage of classical Latin meter—and through it, the plaintive melody of Greek—for a new sound in Hungarian poetry. Here is Berzsenyi:

Oh, how swiftly has winged time suddenly flown away,
All its works afloat round its vanishing feather!
All is appearance, everything under the sky
Fades, as does a forget-me-not.

Radnóti echoes Virgil and Homer in his magnificent dactylic-trochaic hexameters:

> Hail to you, you who keep pace on this wild and mountainous
>   passage,
> blessed old man, are you lifted by wings? or do enemies hunt you?
> Lifted by wings, it is zeal that kindles your eyes into lightnings;
> hail then, O patriarch, now I can see you are one of the ancient
> mighty-wrathed prophets: but tell me, master, which one of them
>   are you?

"The Eighth Eclogue," 1944

The need to refresh the resources of meter to capture the timbre of the poet's personal voice is felt again and again in Hungarian poetry. Endre Ady breaks the rule of exact accent (while keeping the rudder of rhyme) as he breaks the conventions of Hungarian civilization, challenging its frontiers both from France, with its delicate and sensual humanism, and from Hungary's own ancient Asian homeland, with its shamanic Magyar mysticism. Lajos Kassák stretches the line out into a fine Whitmanic or biblical rant, to express the force of modernity:

> Yes! Because out of our ugly stubby fingers fresh force is forking
>   and sprouting,
> and tomorrow will soon drink a pledge on the new walls.
> Tomorrow with iron, asbestos, enormous bulks of granite, we
>   will fling new life on the ruins
> and away with the official State ornamentation! the moonlight!
>   the stagy Orpheums!
> Gigantic skyscrapers we shall build, and for a plaything a replica
>   of the Eiffel Tower.
> Basalt-booted bridges. Onto plazas of steel, steel that sings songs
>   out of the new myths,
> and onto dead railroad-carcasses we hurl fiery screaming
>   locomotives,
> coruscating in their completed orbits, like the eye-paining actinic
>   meteors of the sky.

The spirit of the Italian futurist painters, of Marinetti and Boccione, surely finds here its verbal equivalent. Lines are no longer capitalized, the violence of the times is reproduced in a rhythmical violence that overflows the boundaries of traditional meter. József and Radnóti, among others, experimented with free verse.

But then there was a remarkable turn in Hungarian poetry, for which Mihály Babits may be partly responsible, whereby meter, with all its ability to compress the poet's voice into a form that survives the text, was recovered and revealed as a fit instrument for twentieth-century poetry. Not that free verse was rejected; but unlike in most of the West (and eventually, most of the "civilized" world), free verse was given a place *among* various metrical forms and not promoted to the position of the only acceptable modern form. Babits renewed the classical voice for a thoroughly modern cosmology. In his "Ode on Beauty," the metaphor is of light as information, which in physics is indestructible, passing from star system to star system; but this information is encoded in the poem (even without capitalized lines!) in an elaborately rhymed stanza:

Happier mortals of another star
perhaps will catch that traveling music-light
and read, after some few millennia,
your body-poem's eternal wave-delight.
O may I hope with their hope, when your bright
ray only *then* blossoms in their strange skies,
passing from star to star across the night,
that from your body's holy vessel flies
like precious steam drifting out of a dish of sacrifice.

Your earthly monument may crack and cave,
and the earth too will crumble: mourn, O muse!
for all will crumble, all that nature gave
come to that last ditch and its final ooze;
The ray flies on in space-time's avenues.
Body and soul die: but it cannot die.
This treasure's one that all vast space may use,

and so from star to star it will still fly
into infinity, for the gods to profit by.

And thus poets as modern in esthetics and worldview as Lőrinc Szabó
and Dezső Kosztolányi still have available the old shamanic magic even as
they weave a meaning for the new times. Here is Szabó, with all the fierce
honesty of a D. H. Lawrence but without the slackness of his lines:

> You being you and he being he,
> his interest, not yours, he serves,
> truth just a set of formulae,
> or some state of the nerves;
> and since the outside world won't please,
> and since the masses grant no victories,
> and I'd no say upon the world's decrees,
> it's time for me
> to liberate myself from all of you,
> to loose the bonds, go free.
>
> What am I waiting for so humbly here,
> to glimpse what future times will do?
> time's running, and all life is dear,
> all that's alive is true.
> Either I'm sick, or you are, only one;
> and you tell me I shouldn't watch that gun,
> whether it's love or hate that makes you run,
> and I'm the prey?
> if I'm the understanding one,
> where does that leave me, pray?

And here is Kosztolányi, making a sort of sonic collage, a post-cubist
dithyramb, out of rhymed amphimaceric monometers (to give them their
technical name):

> Feather-light
> Weaver-girl,

Moon and shine
Is your smile,
Sol and fa
Of your name:
Ilona,
Ilona.

Let my soul
Silently
Sing its song,
Lalala,
Lullaby,
Nurse your name,
Ilona,
Ilona.

As it were,
In my ear,
I can hear
Gentle gales,
Weiala,
Mermaid-song,
Swaying souls,
Ilona.

Muezzin
Drones the same
"La Illah
Il' Illah"
As I sing
In your name,
Ilona,
Ilona.

Szabolcs Várady confesses his addiction to the quatrain even as he confesses its anachronism:

Thus I in outworn mode began
my poem, my day—and I can't say
how far I'll get, want to, or can.
And you, will you appear halfway?

As usual, coward, I would dodge.
I hope this antiquated span,
this comfortable measured trudge
may help at least to make it scan.

Or better—dear Lord!—should I say,
I'm rocking in its melody?
Long have my ears preserved its way,
heard as if through eternity.

In other words, the music of a poet's meter is the same thing as the movement of his or her mind. Meter is like those wonderful folds and cutouts that make the pages of a child's pop-up book suddenly leap, when opened, into three dimensions. Meter enables print to speak and sing. The Hungarians realized this when, to a large extent, the rest of western poetry forgot it and forgot much of the music of poetry in its fascination with the visual representation of words on the page. The West's concentration on the printed, as opposed to the spoken, word—which was both a reflection of the technological and economic limitations imposed by paper printing and a consequence of nascent deconstructive theories of écriture—can, I believe, be usefully corrected by the Hungarian example.

How did Hungary escape the trap of paper and print that captures poets, de-faces them, grinds their work into impersonal "morceaux" and reduces them to "author functions"? Three answers present themselves.

One is that the Hungarian poetic "thou" was always maintained among Hungarian poets themselves. Though poets like Ady and Kassák declared themselves to be revolutionaries, they did so as loyal ones: one of Ady's most famous poems, after all, is titled "And I Am Not a Hungarian?" and Kassák's internationalism includes the "poets of Budapest." Radnóti, even while he was being hunted to his death by the very country that he wrote for, declares his solidarity with Ferenc Kazinczy, Vörösmarty, Kosztolányi, Babits, and the other great poets of the tradition. Though for a moment the tormented and tragic Attila József savages his mentor Mihály Babits in a vicious lampoon, he repents afterwards in "Self-Devouring . . . ," one of his most moving poems, in which he accepts the place of the junior artist and fellow-poet despite their political differences. We find Orbán reviving the meter of Balassi's ringing praise-poem of the martial life (though with a different lineation), and Tóth reprising the insanely difficult stanza that József invented for his famous birthday poem. Paradoxically, it is only with these borrowings that the poet's unique mood and feeling can be fully expressed.

All previous—and in some mystical way, all future—poets were interlocutors, friends, intimates to the Hungarian poets. We do not find in Hungarian the contemptuous and final rejections that characterized the darker side of English and French poetry—the English Romantics' contempt for the Augustans, the modernists' dismissal of the Georgians, the symbolistes' hauteur with respect to the Romantics, Eliot's put-down of Milton. Even Ady comes to refresh, not destroy, the Magyar tradition. No Hungarian could have written Tolstoy's inexcusable *What Is Art?* Nor is this tender thou-feeling for other writers confined to fellow Magyars; the Hungarians were great translators, and their sense of personal intimacy extended to Shakespeare, Dante, the French Pléiade, the Roman poets. Gergely, in "Psalm 137," even substitutes János Arany for Jerusalem in her version of that great imprecation. Radnóti's little jokes—taking on the persona of the fictional English poet "Eaton Darr" (the phonemes of his own name reversed), or claiming that his translation of a line by Tibullus was better than the original because Tibullus did not have available the perfect pun in Hungarian—exemplify this intimacy. Arany's magnificent ballad "The Bards of Wales" shows an absolute personal identification with the poets of that distant and ancient rainswept peninsula.

Thus we can see in Magyar poetry extraordinary lineages of themes and poetic ideas, stretching across the centuries, one poet taking up into himself the subjectivity of an earlier master and reworking it in his own way. Chinese Tang poetry does the same thing, but the difference is that Tang poets deepened and enriched a set of inexhaustible genres that were there from the beginning, whereas Magyar poets would invent genres and themes that would be taken up and used by every succeeding poet and sometimes morphed into the beginnings of a new genre. Take, for instance, the Hungarian patriotic poem. From its very beginnings (as, for instance, Kölcsey's "Hymn"), it shows two remarkable characteristics that make it unique: it is composed by the very greatest poets (many nations leave it to second- or third-raters); and it shows an amazing humility and sense of the nation's shame as well as its dear, long-suffering goodness. As the theme develops in various hands, it takes on the idea of Hungary as the tragic protagonist of humanity, as an exemplar of human freedom in general; it is not just "our" flag that is still there, or "Britons" that "never shall be slaves," or "enfants de la patrie," or "Deutschland" that is "über alles," but all humankind. Ady picks up the theme and personifies it (of course) in the mighty River Danube, which then becomes the theme of József's great poem on the subject; and Radnóti generalizes that river into the Nile in his own grand "river of humanity" poem.

Likewise, take those unbroken centuries of the Hungarian love poem. Once the glorious flowering of English love poetry in the sixteenth and seventeenth century was over, love poetry in England never again found more than a sporadic and eccentric recrudescence. But Hungarian love poetry always stood as a personal challenge to later poets—one became the intimate of the dead poets by taking up their ideas and feelings, internalizing them, and reincarnating them in a new century's language. From Balassi through Csokonai, Petőfi, Vörösmarty, Vajda, Kiss, Kaffka, Ady, Heltai, Babits, Arpád Tóth, Szabó, Illyés, Karinthy, Kosztolányi, all the way down to Radnóti, József, Weöres, Nemes Nagy, Gergely, and Krisztina Tóth, there is a continuous handing on of images and ideas and feelings, so that any Radnóti or József or Nemes Nagy love poem is a veritable palimpsest of earlier poems in the genre; the dead poets' live eyes look out, as it were, from the live poet's lines. Radnóti's Fanni, who is a nature spirit or a force of energy animating inanimate objects or an angelic guardian in his poetry, is also Flóra and Ilona and Dandelion and Anna and Kate and Margit Kaffka herself and Margit's little boy Petey and Lilla and Julia.

The same could be said for the other great Hungarian themes—the God of Creation, the elegy for the brother poet, the heroic defeat, the tragic fatalism of desire, the exhilarated moment of epiphany, the frightful and honest confrontation with death or with the sins of the poet, the comical teasing of the beloved, the passionate evocation of the seasons of the year, and so on. It is the tragic loss of that noble tradition—under the pressure of what József rightly called the "monster ideologies" of the twentieth century—that Radnóti mourns in a bitter sonnet:

O Ancient Prisons

O peace of ancient prisons, beautiful
    outdated sufferings, the poet's death,
images noble and heroical,
    which find their audience in measured breath—
how far away you are. Who dares to act
    slides into empty void. Fog drizzles down.
Reality is like an urn that's cracked
    and cannot hold its shape; and very soon
its rotten shards will shatter like a storm.
    What is his fate who, while he breathes, will so
speak of what *is* in measure and in form,
    and only thus he teaches how to know?

    He would teach more. But all things fall apart.
    He sits and gazes, helpless at his heart.

March 27, 1944

In this poem, the imminent and very real murder of the poet himself, which Radnóti had foreseen years before, is folded in to its larger, cultural counterpart—the destruction, by one perverted political modernism or another, of any cultural tradition that stood in the way of its ruling ideology. The ancient prisons are not only the prisons of meter and form, which would soon be discarded in favor of international free verse, but also the prisons of the old genres—the poet's death, the lover's sigh, the well-wrought urn, the poet as bardic truth-teller. Have they been revived once more, or are they still dismissed as nostalgia? *Can* they be revived? This is the challenge for Hungarian poetry, now that it has cast off the monstrous weight of Stalinist lies. Today's poets are taking on the hard work of recovering the thou-feeling for the old poets, for nature, for the great ideas.

A second reason for the survival of the tradition of oral interpersonal immediacy in Hungarian poetry is that in literature the shamanic tradition survived almost intact into modernity, and the shamanic is essentially aural. As McLuhan said, we have no "earlids"; in a live human community, we exist in a constant echoing cave of human sound, including the voices of the dead and of various spirits that we hear in our own heads; there is none of the comfortable distance that visual objectification provides for us. The science of psychology explains away those inner voices—and the spirit voices we hear internally in the conversations of our contemporaries—but they remain, mysterious, around and in us, and are given tongue by poetry. If the practical functions of those voices—the recording of kinship ties and technical procedures and medical techniques and local botanical knowledge, for instance—can be replaced by the institutions of the city or state and their legal and technological systems, then a people can get by without the aural community. But for Hungary it was different: to survive as a community, as a people at all, the Hungarians needed their poets, and needed them not just as remote texts but as charismatic *voices*, renewing both the vital rhythms and the practical vocabulary of the language. Hungary's political and military leadership was routinely annihilated by Turks, Mongols, Austrians, Russians; its genetic inheritance was transformed again and again by intermarriage; and its folkways were diluted by the great ocean of Slavic culture that surrounds the country. All that the Magyars had, to remain Magyars, were their poets.

A third reason for the continuity of the Hungarian "thou," probably closely related to the first two, was the tradition of viva voce (and later, radio and television) poetry recitation. Actors are specially trained in presenting poetry; until very recently schoolchildren memorized astonishing amounts of their nation's finest verse; spoken poetry is a vital part of everyday Hungarian culture. Hungarian poets usually knew each other's work by heart. Hungary's various revolutions against its various oppressors (with the sad exception of the last, successful, one!) were spurred and celebrated by its great poets in mass recitals. Even when print media were censored, poetry survived if it was memorable enough. Thus since metered and rhymed verse is, for various neuropsychological reasons (and as Shakespeare knew), much easier to recite and memorize than prose or free verse, it retained what biologists call an adaptive advantage.

A large part of the future of poetry around the world is now, I believe, bound up in the Internet: a medium superbly equipped to present and disseminate poetry. Electronic text is immediate, live, and active and is already trending back toward the oral and aural. A poem can be on the screen as an actor or accomplished poet/reader recites it, and as visual illustrations or animations give it life. When poetry is oral, it always confronts us in the second person. We may find ourselves turning to Hungary's rich legacy of poetic *performance*, prolonged well into our century and the modern world, as a model to regenerate the vital human community of poetry.

Index